THINKING GUIDE FOR BUSY PEOPLE

Discover How to Avoid Common but Subtle Decision Making Mistakes

HARVEY SMART

Contents

Introduction	v
1. Are You on a Winning Streak?	1
2. Expecting Poor Decisions to Turn Around	12
3. Are You Looking for the Truth ... Or Just Pretending?	22
4. The Two-Options Trap	33
5. Are Your Things Worth That Much?	42
6. Blinded by A Good Impression	50
7. False Causes in Disguise	58
8. The Downside of Playing Safe	69
9. Accepting What Is and Nothing Else	81
10. Feeling Left Out	91
11. Stop and Think Questions	103
Conclusion	111
References	115

© **Copyright 2020 - All rights reserved.**

The content contained within this book may not be reproduced, duplicated or transmitted without direct written permission from the author or the publisher.

Under no circumstances will any blame or legal responsibility be held against the publisher, or author, for any damages, reparation, or monetary loss due to the information contained within this book, either directly or indirectly.

Legal Notice:

This book is copyright protected. It is only for personal use. You cannot amend, distribute, sell, use, quote or paraphrase any part, or the content within this book, without the consent of the author or publisher.

Disclaimer Notice:

Please note the information contained within this document is for educational and entertainment purposes only. All effort has been executed to present accurate, up to date, reliable, complete information. No warranties of any kind are declared or implied. Readers acknowledge that the author is not engaged in the rendering of legal, financial, medical or professional advice. The content within this book has been derived from various sources. Please consult a licensed professional before attempting any techniques outlined in this book.

By reading this document, the reader agrees that under no circumstances is the author responsible for any losses, direct or indirect, that are incurred as a result of the use of the information contained within this document, including, but not limited to, errors, omissions, or inaccuracies.

 Created with Vellum

Introduction

"Life is a matter of choices, and every choice you make makes you."

- John C. Maxwell

The choices we make are often more powerful than we think. Even our smallest decisions can have long-lasting effects in our lives. An apparently trivial decision can trigger a chain of events that can eventually impact our life in a very substantial way. And we also make many automatic decisions, which we repeat over and over again without thinking and whose effects can compound over time and eventually affect our life in a meaningful way. For these reasons, it's important to avoid making poor decisions as much as possible, however small, which is why we need to prevent our cognitive biases from distorting our thinking. This book will help you remove the negative influence of those biases by clarifying what they are, how they influence your thinking, and how to overcome them. However, please keep in mind that this is not a comprehensive textbook that contains all the known cognitive biases because that would make this book impractical and defeat its purpose. My goal was not to write an extensive, boring, college-style psychology textbook that you would take you ages to dissect and understand its content.

Here is how I have structured the book. There are ten chapters in the book and for each chapter, I have described one main cognitive bias, and I have explained how it affects our thinking and decisions in different areas of our lives, such as personal finance, career, relationships, and so on. The book contains examples that illustrate how each main cognitive bias affects us, but for each chapter, I have also provided one primary real life example that shows very clearly how that particular cognitive bias has affected other people who ignored it. In addition to these, each chapter contains two very practical sections. A section called 'Overcoming the… Bias', that explains what actions you can take and what habits you can adopt in order to overcome the main cognitive bias discussed in the chapter. And a section called 'Stop and Think', that contains a series of questions that you can refer to any time you are about to make a decision in order to clarify your thinking and avoid that specific cognitive bias. I hope you find these two sections both practical and valuable.

Once you've finished reading or listening to this book, you will understand the power that your cognitive biases hold over you. You will realize the importance of changing the way you make decisions. You will understand how harmful your cognitive biases can be if you don't stop them from interfering with your thinking. Once you recognize the subtle mistakes that you are making and start correcting them, you will experience positive changes that will add up over time. You will make better decisions in every facet of your life, and these better decisions will lead to better outcomes in your life.

Changing yourself won't happen overnight, though. As you come across new challenges and opportunities in your life and need to make important decisions, you need to remind yourself about the potential dangers of your cognitive biases and take steps to prevent them from interfering with your decisions. You should always refer back to the information in this book if you have any doubts or just want to refresh your memory and make sure that you haven't forgotten anything important.

While there are many things that are beyond our control in life, we can definitely control our thinking. And it's our thinking that determines our decisions. And it's our decisions that lead to our actions. And it's our actions that create our reality. And our reality is the basis of our life on this planet.

I hope you enjoy the book.

ONE

Are You on a Winning Streak?

"Overconfidence precedes carelessness."
Toba Beta

Have you ever reached a point in your life when you just seemed unstoppable? Everything was going your way, and you seemed to make all the right decisions all the time? Well, that is actually a very dangerous position to be in. You must be very careful to keep confidence in check. Most people in this situation use their inflated confidence as a substitute for relevant experience, knowledge and careful analysis. This leads them to make regrettable mistakes that can ruin their careers and lives.

Overconfidence is having an excessive amount of faith in our ability to get things done well, very often within a timeframe. Like with many other things in life, too much of a good thing can become a bad thing. Confidence is good, but being overconfident will make us overestimate our knowledge and skills, which can have very serious consequences in our personal or professional lives.

People's overconfidence has led to disastrous events like the sinking of the Titanic in 1912, the loss of the Challenger space shuttle in 1986, and the mortgage crisis of 2008. In the lead to these events, people placed such a high level of value in their expertise that they could not look at what they were doing objectively. It's okay to believe that we can do something when that belief is based on reality rather than false assumptions about the actual reality.

When we are overconfident, we don't see our shortcomings and are convinced that our judgement is right. This is a dangerous attitude that more often than not affects many other people apart from us. In the most serious situations, people can be physically harmed or even lose their lives due to someone else's overconfidence. This is what happened when Titanic sank, on April 15, 1912, and more than 1,500 people died, while just over 700 people survived. In a press interview in 1907, captain Edward Smith, commander of Titanic, said that he couldn't imagine any conditions which could cause a modern ship to sink. Furthermore, based on his past successful experience with ships smaller than Titanic, he believed that Titanic could be maneuvered to avoid collision with any iceberg after establishing visual contact with the iceberg. For these reasons, Titanic's speed wasn't relaxed and the lookout for icebergs wasn't increased, which made the collision inevitable.[1]

While the sinking of Titanic is an event from the distant past, overconfidence keeps making thousands of victims every year across the entire world. Many serious accidents happen as a direct result overconfidence, mostly on the road. Every year, several thousand people lose their lives in car accidents caused by speeding drivers overconfident in their ability to control their cars at high speeds. In 2017, for example, 9,717 people lost their lives in the US in car crashes caused by speeding. That's the equivalent of over 6 Titanics sinking in one year, and that number doesn't include the people who died in accidents caused by alcohol-impaired drivers, which arguably suffer from an alcohol induced overconfidence when crashing their cars.[2]

Overconfidence can affect many aspects of our lives and have consequences which can vary from small and short-lived in some situations to very serious and long lasting in others. It can destroy our finances if we make careless or very risky investments, or if we constantly spend more money than we can afford. It can ruin a great career opportunity for us if we don't prepare properly for a job interview. It can cause us to fail important projects if we take them on without being competent enough to run them successfully. And it can also cause us to get seriously ill and end up in hospital or even die if we ignore our unhealthy habits or if we neglect to protect ourselves against deadly viruses, like Covid-19.

A very notorious example of an overconfident person in dealing with the Covid-19 pandemic, who later turned into an overly cautious individual after his personal encounter with the virus, is the UK prime minister, Boris Johnson. When the pandemic started to spread in the UK, in early March 2020, he dismissed the Covid-19 infection as something very similar to the seasonal flu and nothing to worry too much about. However, on March 27, the prime minister tested positive for coronavirus and his health aggravated within days. He had to be hospitalized on April 5 because his symptoms were persistent and he was moved to intensive care the following day, and given oxygen to help him breathe. His condition deteriorated so fast that his doctors put together a plan to deal with his potential death. He spent three nights in the intensive care unit, then he was moved back to a normal hospital ward and discharged from hospital a few days later, on April 12. After his personal battle with the Covid-19 infection, the UK prime minister's attitude towards the dangers of Covid-19 has changed markedly and understandably so.[3]

Some common ways in which overconfidence can hurt your career and your finances include: taking jobs that you are not properly qualified for, starting a business in a field you know very little about, or starting a business in a field you are very knowledgeable about but wanting to do everything by your own and refusing to partner up with other people with complementary experience and skills.

If you rush to take a new job that appears to be exciting, although you know that you don't meet all the key requirements, but you still feel very confident that you can quickly upgrade your knowledge and skills to be successful in this new role, you may end up in a very stressful situation, learning and doing things that you don't like at all and eventually failing in the new job. This situation can be particularly stressful in a fast-paced environment, when you are against tight deadlines which you need to meet while trying to figure out how exactly to do your job properly in that new setting. What seems easy in theory, it is often more difficult and complicated in real life.

Similarly, starting a business in a field you have little or no knowledge in because you are very confident that you can do it successfully can also turn out to be a bad decision if you don't know what issues to expect and how to deal with those issues effectively. It is, of course, possible to venture in a completely new field and build a successful business without having any prior experience in that particular field. However, your chances of success are higher, the more cautious you are, and lower, the more overconfident you are. Opening a restaurant is a good example of a business that seems easy enough for many people with some prior business experience to try, and many of them fail because they make poor decisions because they don't know the subtleties and complexities of running a successful restaurant. They just assume it's easy, based on their experience as customers, but this is just a false assumption that can lead to failure.

Even when starting a business in a field you actually know very well, overconfidence can also cause you many problems, which could eventually lead you to failure if you are not very careful. In these situations, it's often tempting to become a solopreneur and try to do everything by yourself for too long, especially if you are afraid to share your new product or business idea with others because you think they may steal it from you and start competing with you from a stronger basis, having significantly more resources and money available to invest in the new product or business idea than you do. The problem is that in real life, when you start a new business, especially in technology, the number of tasks you need to perform and problems that you need to solve can grow out of control in a very short time and you will end up being overwhelmed and unable to do anything properly. An added difficulty for a solopreneur working mostly by themselves is switching between different tasks and business functions. For example, if you are a solopreneur currently focused on running a marketing campaign but need to fix an urgent bug or add an extra feature to the app that you are building as your product because every user is asking for it, it actually takes time for you to get back into the code, remember how it's all put together, and then figure out how to fix the bug or build the new feature. And if something goes wrong with the marketing campaign while you are busy coding, most likely, you won't catch that problem either. There are many negative implications stemmed from overloading your plate as a solopreneur and you need to be aware of all the main ones in order to be successful.

We can become a victim of our own overconfidence in two ways. Either by taking on single tasks which seem doable to us but which we prove incapable of doing or by taking on multiple tasks which we are capable of handling individually, but not all at the same time. For example, if you are overconfident in the workplace, you can end up taking on too much work by always saying yes to your boss or to your customers. As a result, you overload yourself with too many responsibilities and won't be able to deliver everything on time and at the expected quality. So you will end up cutting corners, missing your deadlines, delivering poor quality work, even completely forgetting about some of your commitments, and in the end you will disappoint your boss, your company and your customers and may end up losing your job.

So, you need to do your research and make sure you have realistic expectations before taking on a new job or starting a new business, however exciting those may seem initially. You don't want your dream job or dream business to turn into a nightmare, right? Just because something looks easy, it doesn't automatically mean it is. It could also mean that you are fooling yourself or that you have been misled by someone.

Another major drawback of overconfidence is that we stop learning new things and improving ourselves. After all, we don't need to learn anything at all if we think we know enough already, right? For this reason, overconfidence is a very unhealthy attitude which keeps us stuck in our current situation and prevents us from making the right decisions and making progress in our lives. Additionally, overconfidence makes us come across as arrogant and unpleasant, which can have a negative impact on our personal and professional lives as our friends, family and peers will probably start avoiding us.

The opposite of overconfidence is lack of confidence. This opposite attitude has one major downside to it because it prevents many otherwise capable people from achieving their true potential in their personal and professional lives. People who lack confidence tend to either overthink or over-prepare for an opportunity until it's too late. Most of these people also believe that they are never good enough and that they will never be ready for what they keep preparing for.

Because overconfidence can set you up for massive failure in high-risk situations, while lack of confidence can lead to missed opportunities, the key to success in any new endeavors is to find the middle point between these two extremes.

Overconfidence in the Real World

Nick Adams is a descendant of one of America's founding fathers and was once a successful investor with Wellington Management. His success came from investing consistently in traditional bank stock, which earned him 28% annual returns. If he continued on this path, he probably would have remained successful with his returns. However, he wanted to try his hand at something new.

He decided to pour hundreds of millions of dollars into two tech start-up companies, Mozido, Inc. and Powa Technologies Group, LLC. Mozido designs, develops, and provides mobile commerce and payment solutions on a global scale. Powa was known for its commerce, e-commerce and mobile commerce services. With the online revolution occurring, tech-based companies like this seemed like a solid investment for most people. Mr. Adams told other investors the companies were continuing to grow more valuable, and many of them heeded his advice and invested.

Reports came out later showing that these two tech companies were actually losing millions of dollars and had very low revenue when Nick Adams invested in them. Powa Technologies actually ended up filing for bankruptcy in 2016. The company had blown through about $200 million worth of investor capital. Mozido lost major sums as well.

Most big-time investors and entrepreneurs don't mind taking risks to help increase their wealth. This is okay if the risk is calculated. For a calculated risk to occur, the individual must practice a healthy level of confidence. Mr. Adams, on the other hand, allowed his past success to go to his head, not realizing that past wins do not guarantee future success. He became overconfident with his predictions.

Mr. Adams' overconfidence and lack of essential research led him to lose billions of dollars for himself and Wellington Management. Some estimates put the loss amount at $6 billion. This was about a 40% decrease in his company's portfolio value from when the company was at its peak in 2014. This financial blunder was thoroughly described in a Wall Street Journal article in 2017. Mr. Adams ended up calling the investment the worst mistake in his 30-plus year investing career.[4]

Overcoming the Overconfidence Bias

Given how dangerous overconfidence can be, it is paramount to avoid allowing it to bias our most important decisions. Sometimes we can make a quick recovery from a bad decision caused by overconfidence, learn a lesson and move on, but not always. In many circumstances, overconfidence can lead us into serious trouble that can have a long-term impact on our lives, and for this reason it's important for us to cultivate habits that can help us avoid its negative influence. Here are few things you can do to prevent the overconfidence bias from affecting your decisions.

KNOW **The Worst-Case Scenario And Take Calculated Risks**

When it comes to venturing into a new project or experience, it is foolish to take risks without proper preparation. So, before making a 'go' or 'no go' decision, you must clarify several things in advance. You must determine what could go wrong and how likely it is for things to go wrong. You also need to figure out what to do if things go wrong. And most importantly, you need to know exactly what's the worst that could happen, and whether you can afford or you can recover from the worst-case scenario if things go terribly wrong. To succeed in life at any level, you must be willing to take a certain amount of risk, but it must be a calculated risk that you can manage successfully.

BE **Humble**

While an overconfident person often comes across as arrogant, a merely confident and down-to-earth person often comes across as humble. They do not sing their own praises and allow other people, as well as their work, to speak for them. There is an adage that states something like, "Michael Jordan is the greatest of all time because he does not have to tell you that he is." Rarely, if ever, will you see Michael Jordan out there telling everyone he is the greatest. Other people do it for him. Having a humble attitude allows you to slow down, get a better understanding of the tasks ahead and the risks involved, be realistic about any gaps in your knowledge and skills, acknowledge these gaps without worrying that you are losing face by being honest with yourself and others, ask for help from others when needed, avoid any foreseeable risks and mistakes and maximize your chances of success. Having a humble attitude will also make it easier for you to admit your own mistakes and learn from them.

GET **An Expert Opinion**

Because the main issue with overconfidence is failing to realize that there is a perilous gap between what we can do and what needs to be done, we need an objective way to confirm whether we have everything it takes to be successful in what we are trying to achieve or not. The best way to do this is to consult with people who are experts in the area that we are interested in. These people, who are also known as subject-matter experts, can help us understand the critical success factors, the risks involved, the hidden costs, the true financial investment needed for success, what key professionals we must hire to complement our skills and increase our chances of success, and so on. Where can you find the subject-matter experts to validate your assumptions and provide you with all these insights? You can find them by talking to your friends, peers and business partners and also online, as many of them have their own websites, podcasts and blogs, and have also published books on Amazon, courses on Udemy and Coursera, videos on YouTube, and answers on Quora.

Having the right level of confidence is key to make the right decisions in life. You need enough confidence to take the opportunities that can benefit you and move forward in life.

But you also need to be realistic about your knowledge and skills and avoid jumping on opportunities that you are not ready for and that can actually hurt you to a large extent.

Stop and Think

When you are on a winning streak, going from one success to another, getting everything right, and about to make a very important decision, ask yourself:

- What exactly makes me feel so sure that I am making the right decision now?
- Is my decision based on sufficient and relevant information?
- Am I cutting any corners or jumping to conclusions?
- Who can I speak to in order to validate my assumptions?
- Do I know all the potential risks?
- Does anyone disagree with me? Do they have a valid point? Have I dismissed their views too quickly and without proper consideration?
- Are there any hidden costs or additional costs further down the line that I am not aware of?
- Is there anything important that I could be missing?
- Do I have enough experience and knowledge to make an informed decision in this particular instance?

TWO

Expecting Poor Decisions to Turn Around

"Some of us think holding on makes us strong, but sometimes it is letting go."
Hermann Hesse

Have you ever forced yourself to eat food that you didn't really like simply because you already cooked it or paid for it? It happens to all of us, even though it makes no rational sense to make ourselves uncomfortable or even sick by eating food we don't like. We could just throw it out and eat something else that we would enjoy more, but no, we just don't like wasting that food, do we?

The **sunk cost fallacy** happens when we continue to invest time, money, or any other resources in a project or activity for the sake of our past investments rather than because it makes rational sense to continue to do so.

We can see the sunk cost fallacy as a mental disconnect between paying for something and not getting the expected benefit in return. This means that we are so determined to get what we paid for that we will continue to pursue it long after we have realized that we are not getting what we paid for. To put it simply, it's an ongoing commitment to an initial investment.

The sunk cost fallacy affects all aspects of our lives. We commit to our investments, beliefs, traditions, people, careers, and circumstances and then stay committed to them even after this commitment has become detrimental to us. When we are in this position, we seek to justify the efforts we have already made and continue to make similar efforts, regardless of the outcome. The consequences of our sunk cost fallacies are often minor and short-lived, such as the example of eating a meal you don't really like, but they can also be dire and long-lasting.

In business, a sunk cost refers to money that has already been spent and cannot be recovered. Sunk costs should never be the driving reason for a business to keep spending money on ongoing or existing projects, products or assets that the business owns. The driving reason should be the financial benefits from those projects, products or assets.

Let's take a hypothetical example. Let's assume that a business decided to invest $1 million in a project that was expected to generate $1 million in profit within a year. However, halfway through the project, after half a million dollars has been invested, the market conditions have changed and the expected profit has dropped to zero. This means that the project no longer makes any commercial sense. The money which has been invested already is a sunk cost and it should not be used to justify spending another half a million dollars to complete the project. This would be a complete waste of time and money. Unfortunately, in many cases like this, businesses continue to invest additional money, mostly for the sake of the money which has already been invested, but also because people who made the very first decision to invest are unwilling to acknowledge making a bad call and abandon an unfinished project.

The sunk cost fallacy generally refers to money which we have already invested in material things and which we can't recover, but it can also refer to other resources such as time and effort and also to investments in relationships, not just material things. We tend to stay in unhappy relationships with friends or romantic partners long after they have started troubling us. The time, effort and emotions which we have invested in these relationships make it very difficult for us to move away from them.

The sunk cost fallacy hurts us twice. When we stay committed to something that causes us harm, not only are we suffering from that thing, but we are also being prevented from taking other opportunities. Let's take a simple example of watching a movie at the cinema. If you go to the cinema to watch a movie which seemed interesting to you, but you don't really enjoy it and you are still watching it until the very end just because you have paid for it, then you are missing the opportunity of doing something more pleasurable, instead of being uncomfortable for a couple of hours or so. Or, if we take a romantic relationship as an example. If you are in an unhappy relationship, you could be wasting your time on someone who brings you very little joy, instead of moving on and finding a more suitable partner, with whom you could have great chemistry and be truly happy.

There are several reasons why we get trapped in the sunk cost fallacy. We hate making mistakes; we hate admitting our mistakes; we hate wasting money and time; we value commitments; we get attached emotionally; we have a hard time letting go, and we fail to see and accept any alternative options.

From childhood, we are often taught that it is not okay to make mistakes. We learn this from our parents, teachers, coaches and many other influential adults in our lives. We may have been punished for our small mistakes. This taught us that it's never okay to be wrong or to fail. As a result, we have a desire to always be right and to always succeed. This desire leads us to fail to see and accept our mistakes and to hold on to them, no matter how bad things get.

Speaking of childhood, most of us have siblings and grew up in families with limited financial resources. Because money was in limited supply, it had to be spent very carefully and never wasted, and for this reason we hate wasting our money, even small amounts. After all, we all know from a very early age that money doesn't grow on trees, don't we?

Commitment is yet another factor that explains our sunk cost fallacies. Society as a whole values commitment. We see it as a sign of strength, integrity, and intelligence, but this is only true when we commit to things which are positive and valuable. Otherwise, it's a sign of weakness, blindness, or ignorance. We should always reconsider our commitment to anything that is hurting us or not helping us. As the quote at the beginning of the chapter suggests, sometimes we are better and stronger by letting go.

Finally, the bigger our emotional investments in something, the harder it becomes for us to abandon it and to overcome our sunk cost fallacy.[5] We all know that when our judgement is tainted by our emotions, it becomes difficult for us to make the right decisions and also to act on them. Outside observers can see things more clearly than us in these situations, but only when they are not invested emotionally, otherwise their judgment will also be biased.

The opposite of the sunk cost fallacy is called **the shiny object syndrome**. This means being too quick to abandon your current investments even if they are still valuable and worth keeping, just to rush to buy the next promising thing or jump on to the next promising project. The decision to move on, in this case, is based almost entirely on the promised benefits and on a very superficial understanding of the actual effort needed to succeed. The shiny object syndrome will be discussed in more detail in Chapter 10.

The Sunk Cost Fallacy in the Real World

The supersonic Concorde aircraft might be the poster child for the sunk cost fallacy. If you're not familiar with this story, it was a British-French turbojet that operated between 1976 and 2003. A total of 20 were built, and only two airlines ended up using them. The speed of the aircraft plus the luxury services offered made the flights very expensive, to the point that only wealthy individuals flew on them. The cost of a flight ranged anywhere from $4,000 to $8,000 on average, but it sometimes cost much more. Also, the speed at which the aircraft traveled created a sonic boom, which was not appropriate when it came to flying over crowded metropolitan areas. As a result, the only travel possible for the Concorde was over the ocean. Such a plane, as you might expect, costs a lot of money. The original investment was about $2 billion.

Unfortunately, due to the limited number of people flying, the return on investment did not justify the original cost. The Concorde did not turn out to be the commercial success its creators hoped for. Because of the investments that were already made, the UK and French governments continued to fund the project, even though there was no economic case for it. Of course, they continued to lose more money on it. Eventually, they were forced to stop using these planes after a fatal crash that killed more than 100 people. Any credibility the aircraft had was gone by this point. Considering the project cost French and UK taxpayers $1.5 to $2 billion before the first plane ever even took off, it is unimaginable to think how many billions were ultimately lost after over 20 years of flight.[6]

Overcoming the Sunk Cost Fallacy

Don't be a victim of the sunk cost fallacy. You can at least limit its influence on your thinking and start making better decisions in your day to day life. Here are a few steps that you can take in order to overcome the sunk cost fallacy.

KEEP In Mind That Not All Promising Ideas Succeed

Not everything you buy or invest in will turn out to be a good decision, regardless of how much effort you put into your research and analysis. This is a fact of life. We live in a very complex world of countless events and interactions, and it's virtually impossible to make the right decisions all the time. Plus, we make many of our decisions based on limited information because we don't have the time and resources necessary to do more research and make better decisions. Plus, in many instances, we just need a quick decision.

For these reasons, it's normal that some of our decisions will go wrong, but we need to be honest with ourselves when this happens. And sometimes it's our fault because we made a poor decision based on the right information, but sometimes it's not our fault at all because we made the right decision based on the right information but things have changed since then and what it looked like a promising idea turned into a poor idea.

NEVER GET FIXATED On How Much You Have Invested Already

This is the primary cause for the sunk cost fallacy, focusing on the cost to justify a poor buying or investment decision that costs us even more if we stick to it. You should always keep in mind the very reasons why you have spent your money and your time on something in the first place. What were you expecting you to get in return for your money or your time? Did you get it or not? Was it worth your investment or not? Never lose sight of those initial expectations and if they haven't been met, accept that it was a bad idea in hindsight, cut your losses and move on.

DEFINE Your Exit Criteria From The Beginning

When you decide to invest a significant amount of time, money or any other resources in something promising, it's always best to define your exit criteria and strategy if things go wrong. You can do this at any time but it's best to do it at the very beginning. This way, you will know exactly when to get out and how to get out if things don't go as expected and you don't run the risk of getting carried away, losing sight of the big picture, over-investing significant amounts of money and time and becoming a victim of the sunk cost fallacy.

People who are investing in the stock market use an exit technique called a stop-loss to limit their losses if their investments go wrong. It's a relatively simple but effective way for them to define and implement an exit criteria and avoid the sunk cost fallacy. A stop-loss works in the following way. When an investor buys shares in a company expecting those shares to go up in price over time and make a profit, they also create a stop-loss order to limit their losses if the share price goes down, unexpectedly, instead of up. This happens quite often due to unforeseen events. Without the stop-loss order, the investor could lose a significant amount of money if he is not very careful.

To illustrate how a stop-loss works, let's assume an investor buys 1,000 shares in Apple at $100 dollars per share, and has decided to set up his stop-loss price at $90. Let's say, the share price goes up to $110, but then Apple disappoints its investors by launching a series of lackluster products which causes the share price to drop and keep dropping to $80 per share. Without the stop-loss, this investor could have lost $20 per share, which is $20,000 in total. But because he set up the stop-loss, he sold his shares at $90 per share and only lost $10 per share, which is $10,000 in total, instead of $20,000.

Here is another example of an exit criteria. Let's say you are invited to a party on Friday evening by someone you barely know. You don't know anyone else at the party apart from your new friend who invited you. You could, in this case, decide in advance that you will be there for an hour and then leave if you don't have a great time, and do something else instead. If the party is great, then you stay and enjoy it. If it isn't, you leave and don't suffer by being in the company of people you have nothing in common with.

KEEP **Your Emotions Out Of Your Material Decisions**

When it comes to material decisions, it's best to let go of any emotional attachments or avoid them in the first place if possible. You can avoid letting your emotions interfere with your decisions by using a pre-defined exit criteria, as explained above. Alternatively, you can ask a few people, who won't be affected by your decision in any way, for their opinion and recommendation and rely on their feedback to make a more rational decision.

Sometimes, it may be very difficult to keep your emotions out of your decisions, especially if you have put your heart and soul into a project. In that case, it's best to take some time off, get some distance, and think of alternatives and maybe potential solutions that you could still try as the last resort.

The sunk cost fallacy is a very common cognitive bias that affects our personal and professional lives. Whether its impact on our lives is big or small, it's better to always keep an eye on it and minimize its consequences as much as possible. As the saying goes, "Don't throw good money after bad."

When a promising idea turns into a poor idea, accept the current reality, accept your initial mistake or that things have changed in the meantime, learn your lesson, cut your losses and move on. This is how you avoid the sunk cost fallacy.

Stop and Think

When you are in a situation where investing more money and/or time brings you no further benefits and it could even hurt you, ask yourself:

- Why am I doing this, anyway? Is it for the sake of the money and time I have invested already?
- Would I be better off by cutting my losses and moving on?

- What other opportunities would I miss by sticking to this path?

As a matter of principle, try to avoid making a bad investment even worse by investing any additional resources like money or time.

THREE

Are You Looking for the Truth ... Or Just Pretending?

"Most people do not really want the truth. They just want reassurance that what they believe is the truth."
Anonymous

Have you ever bought a product on Amazon that you found disappointing? When thinking about your purchase, did you later realize that you had simply ignored all the negative reviews and comments and focused mostly on the positive ones? You did this because you loved the idea of the product and chose to believe only the positive reviews that supported your desired outcome. Ignoring the other side of the story, so to speak, resulted in a bad decision in the end.

The **confirmation bias** causes us to only search for or only pay attention to information that reinforces our previously held beliefs while ignoring any evidence that contradicts those beliefs.

We can also see the confirmation bias as a selection bias in the collection of evidence to support our point of view. As people, we naturally want to feel good about ourselves and we also like to be right. For these reasons, we are motivated to select the evidence that confirms our point of view and ignore all the evidence that contradicts it, which then leads us to false conclusions and poor decisions. The obvious issue with the confirmation bias is the fact that we close ourselves off to valid information. This heavily limits our way of thinking and can even be dangerous in some instances.

Let's look at an example of the confirmation bias. It is the year 2020, and we are currently facing the COVID-19 pandemic that has shaken up the world. As the virus started spreading in more and more countries at very alarming rates, and nationwide lockdowns were introduced to stop the virus, a major controversy started occupying the minds of people. This controversy was over whether people should wear face masks or not. The experts were divided and so were governments and the public. Governments in different countries varied in their approach. Some were pro-mask and strict, making face masks compulsory in all public places, both indoors and outdoors, like the Spanish government. Others, like the British government, were almost anti-mask and relaxed, stating that the face masks were not actually recommended because they hadn't been proven to stop the spread of the virus.

What was very noticeable in this debate was that people on both sides of the debate were very vocal and focused exclusively on the reasons why their position was correct. Some medical experts claimed that masks were not effective in stopping the spread of the virus. They said people wearing face masks touched their face often to reposition it, thereby increasing the risk of infection, and that they forgot to wash their hands and got too close to other people since they had a false sense of security. If people respected both the social distancing and the hand hygiene very strictly, then the masks were pointless, they said. On the other side of the argument, other medical experts said masks prevent people from expelling infectious droplets onto other people or areas which greatly reduce the risk of transmitting the disease to others. When used properly in conjunction with social distancing and good hand hygiene, masks were very effective at reducing the spread of COVID-19, these experts said. Most people adopted one of the two views and refused to consider any information that was counter to their established view.

Unsurprisingly, the confirmation bias is very pervasive in politics. As time goes by, we seem to become more divided simply because we can't see the other person's side amidst our distorted judgment. So many people choose a political party and then look only at evidence that suggests their candidates are great while the ones from the other side are the so much worse. You may have noticed that people conveniently leave out a candidate's past misdeeds when it's someone they like and support, but they are happy to talk about the misdeeds of the person they dislike and don't support. If people could simply look beyond party lines and end the confirmation bias related to it, they would see both the negative and positive attributes that both sides bring to the table and form an objective opinion about candidates and political parties. By doing this, we could close the divide that we have created in politics and in society, or at least have a better understanding of the issues we are facing and of other people's views.

There are many factors that contribute to our confirmation biases, that either strengthen or create them in the first place. These include, having the desire to always be right and never wrong, having a big ego, relying on other people's thinking, avoiding the mental effort that is necessary to consider any information that contradicts our beliefs, having a people pleasing attitude or wanting to avoid any potential conflicts with other people, having a very strong positive or negative frame of mind that distorts our perception and prevents us from seeing and understanding the truth, long-held beliefs, being passionate about a topic, etc.

A very significant factor that contributes to the creation and reinforcement of our confirmation biases is our tendency to gravitate towards people who think the same way we do while avoiding people who think differently. Sadly, we even avoid some of our friends and family members because they think very differently about certain topics than us. Of course, there are instances when we can't ignore or minimize the importance of the differences between us and other people, but often we just lose sight of the bigger picture and focus only on those differences. Imagine how many wonderful relationships are missed out on because people get fixated on what separates them instead of concentrating on what they have in common and brings them together.

There is another cognitive bias that relates to what we have been discussing. It is called the **choice-supportive bias.** This bias makes it so that once a decision is made, people tend to over-focus on its benefits and minimize its flaws. The key difference between the confirmation bias and the choice-supportive bias is that the confirmation bias makes people ignore contradictory information, while the choice supportive bias makes people minimize its importance. People can be indecisive, but when they decide, it is hard to change their minds.

The opposite of the confirmation bias is to have an open mind and always seek and consider all evidence. This requires more time, effort and patience, but it ensures that you always know the truth or are as close as possible to the truth and know how to support your arguments while competently refuting your opponents' arguments. It also requires you to be open to changing your mind when you discover that your previously held beliefs are wrong.

Confirmation Bias in the Real World

A good example of confirmation bias in the real world is the argument between creationists and evolutionary biologists about the age of the Earth. Many creationists believe that the Earth is only 6,000 years old, which is an estimate based on the Bible. However, scientists have used modern technology called radiometric dating to measure the radioactive decay of various elements within rocks to help determine its age. Using radiometric dating on a multitude of elements, the scientists determined that the Earth is approximately 4.54 billion years old. This is a massive difference compared to the 6,000 years suggested by creationists. Despite these facts, most creationists deny any evidence based on science and simply state it was planted there by God just to test our beliefs.

Another real-life example of confirmation bias is the practice of homeopathy. This is based on the idea that the body has the ability to completely heal itself using only minute amounts of highly diluted substances. Original experiments by Jacque Benveniste studied the effect of histamines on the body. He determined, based on his own research, that diluting these histamines would increase their effectiveness in the body and boosts the immune system effectively protecting the body from various diseases.

The problem was that the experiment was not done properly. Due to the lack of a blind study, there was a placebo effect observed. Benveniste ignored any evidence from other scientists that contradicted what he believed. Believers in homeopathy continued to spread the false benefits of the practice, and today a wide array of people still believe in its effects, despite mounting evidence to the contrary.[7]

Overcoming The Confirmation Bias

The confirmation bias affects most of us, and it often affects many areas of our lives, rather than just one. When we refuse to see or just ignore any contradictory information about a topic, we can't possibly have a good understanding of that topic. Even if the contradictory information is not strong enough to change our minds, we should at least be aware of it and know for sure that it's not sufficient to change our opinion. With this in mind, here are few things that you can do to overcome the confirmation bias.

KEEP An Open Mind

It takes a certain level of bravery to keep an open mind and be willing to consider information that challenges our views but you must do it if you truly want to overcome the confirmation bias. The more passionate we are about a topic, the harder it is for us to keep our minds open and take into account any contradictory information that we may come across. Especially if we have spent years or even decades defending and strengthening our position on that particular topic.

However, it is necessary to keep an open mind to make sure we understand the full picture which will help us think more deeply about the subject we are interested in and form an informed opinion about it. And if this will make us change our minds based on evidence which is new to us, then there is nothing wrong with that. It would be foolish for us to stick to an old belief if we came across information that invalidates it. After all, all the great minds in the history of mankind became great because they kept an open mind and looked carefully into all the information that contradicted the existing beliefs. Imagine if all scientists, doctors, and philosophers who lived on this planet were strongly influenced by the confirmation bias. If they had not challenged society's ingrained beliefs, we would still think the earth is flat and not have a cure for many diseases.

TRUST Your Own Thinking

We all look up to experts and coaches and very successful people and rely on their knowledge and advice, but once we have reached a sound level of understanding of a topic, we must start relying on our own thinking as well. We all come from different places, have different backgrounds, and because of this we see things from different perspectives. Additionally, some of the people who influence us may not be up to date with the latest developments and latest knowledge in their area of expertise, and for this reason some of their advice may not be valid anymore. Finally, when someone is successful in one area, keep in mind that their success has been achieved in a context that most likely won't be available to you and me. Our circumstances will probably be different, and their knowledge and advice may not work for us at all if the circumstances are not the same or very similar.

When evaluating your own opinion and those of others, always look through the lens of the facts. Unfortunately, as you know, you can't trust everything you hear in the media, or from other people. There is a great deal of fake news these days, and lots of hidden agendas at play. You must feel confident about questioning other people's point-of-view and even yours when it doesn't seem quite right. Always do with your own independent research to make sure that you are making your decisions based on the best available information.

AVOID BEING OVERLY Negative Or Overly Positive

A strong negative or positive frame of mind strengthens our confirmation bias, and its impact is very easy to notice by the people surrounding us. When we are in a strong negative frame of mind, we often fail to see any positive opportunities that could improve our situation, even when they are very obvious to everyone else. Most likely, other people will notice those opportunities first and then draw our attention to them. However, some people are so pessimistic that they may even turn all those positives, that others are telling them about, into negatives or be very skeptical that any of those positive things can ever work for them. On the other hand, a strong positive frame of mind can prevent us from seeing dangerous situations, which others can see clearly. Therefore, you must avoid these two extreme frames of mind as much as possible, and if you find yourself in one of them, you must make a sustained effort to get out of it so that you don't miss any important information.

CONTROL YOUR EGO

It is okay to have pride in what you do and who you are, but don't let your ego prevent you from changing and growing. Learn how to leave your ego at the proverbial door. Unfortunately, the stronger your opinions, the bigger your ego is, which increases your confirmation bias. When what you know becomes part of your own identity, then you will perceive any contradictory information as a personal attack and will either avoid the contradictory information or not accept it as true.

When you believe you already have all the right information, it can be hard to consider any views that contradict yours. Remind yourself that the things you know can sometimes be wrong and that's okay. Practice humility and be kind to yourself for not having all the answers. Humility allows you to listen to others intently and understand what they are saying. Doing this will not affect your intelligence or your ego in any negative way. On the contrary, because you gather a wider range of information and make more informed decisions, this habit will make you smarter. You will also start seeing and understanding things from other points of view which builds empathy with other people. Learn to control your ego so you can learn more and overcome the confirmation bias.

BE Careful About Voicing Your Disagreements

When you come across information that contradicts people's entrenched beliefs, you need to be careful about talking about your discovery with others, at least initially. Disagreeing with people can have very negative consequences in our lives, which can vary from very small to very significant and from temporary to permanent, and for these reasons we should always be cautious about voicing our disagreements. Sadly, our honest opinion is not always valued and in fact many people who ask us for our opinion are actually hoping for a positive reply and get very upset with us if we disagree instead. Most married guys will probably relate to this statement, right? 'Killing' the messenger who delivers bad news is still very common in our society. Having said that, the fear of negative consequences should never discourage you from forming your own opinions in disagreement with other people. Just be careful about revealing them to others who may instantly dislike you for doing so, and then harbor negative feelings and seek revenge.

The truth is that we can't always agree with somebody on everything they say or think. If your relationship with someone becomes tense because you have discovered that you have different views on something, ask the other person to agree to disagree on that particular topic and take a break from discussing it. You can try to have a more rational discussion and get a better understanding of your differences later, in a calm manner. But use your subsequent discussions on that topic to get a clear understanding of each other's points of view instead of exchanging insults and jumping to conclusions.

To avoid the confirmation bias and make sound decisions in your life, you should always take into account any contradictory information and consider it carefully before deciding whether it matters or not and whether it's strong enough to change your initial belief. And you should never be afraid to change your beliefs or disagree with others based on new evidence, but you should be careful about speaking your mind to avoid upsetting people who have the power to silence you or hurt you in any way.

Stop and Think

When you come across a new piece of information that contradicts one of your existing beliefs, ask yourself:

- Is this true?
- Can I trust this source?
- How significant is this new piece of information?
- Does it change anything at all?
- Who is going to win and who is going to lose if this is true?

- Could anyone lose their power, job or reputation based on this information?
- Would anyone's ego get seriously hurt?

When everything that you hear or read about a topic you care about reinforces what you already believed to be true, ask yourself:

- Is this the full picture or just carefully cropped out version of the truth that people keep repeating without much thinking?
- What if all these people are wrong?
- Can the opposite be true?
- Are my assumptions still true today?
- What is the actual proof that my beliefs are right?
- Who disagrees with my beliefs and why?
- Has anything changed since I made my mind up about this?
- Why exactly do I believe things as I do?

FOUR

The Two-Options Trap

"Arm yourself with as many options as possible before making your next move."
Mallory Ortberg

Have you ever been offered a choice between two options and didn't realize that an even better one was possible but not mentioned?

A **false dichotomy** happens when only two choices are presented to us, although other choices are possible. False dichotomies are usually characterized by "either this or that" language and result from an omission of choices, which can be intentional or unintentional.[8]

A **false dilemma** is very similar to a false dichotomy. The only difference is that a dilemma gives you two choices that are both unattractive.

When we are given only two options, then it follows that we must choose one of them. We may not like either choice in front of us, but we have to pick one in order to move forward. This type of thinking negates the possibility that there are other options that are viable. But we are so focused on the two options in front of us that we can't see any other ones. Our tunnel vision prevents us from seeing any other alternatives, so we have no idea of their existence.

It has happened to most of us to be presented with only two choices during arguments, ultimatums or as a negotiating tactic. People use false dichotomies against us either intentionally, to gain an unfair advantage, or unintentionally. It is our job to recognize when this is happening. False dichotomies force us to take extreme positions. As a result, we end up making poor decisions that negatively affect our lives and benefit the other person.

Here are some examples of possible false dichotomies that you may have come across.

- "If you are not my friend, then you are my enemy." This suggests that there is no room for neutrality.
- "If you are not part of the solution, then you are part of the problem." There are many interpretations of solution and problem. There is more than one way to address things.
- "We either do this, or we are doomed." This suggests that there is no other viable course of action.

Very often, we don't question the false dichotomies that we come across in our lives because we are convinced, based on our culture or prior knowledge, that only two options are possible, like in the examples above. But this is rigid thinking, and it doesn't help us make the best decisions in our lives. In those situations in which we automatically think that only two choices are possible, we should check whether more choices could be possible. As a matter of principle, if the stakes are high, we should always look beyond the obvious options regardless of how many we know of.

It's also common to encounter false dichotomies when we are under pressure to make a quick decision. The time pressure could sometimes be avoidable, though. If we have an urgent need for something, then we know that the time pressure is real and probably unavoidable. But, if we are merely pressurized into making a decision by someone else, for example, a very eager salesperson, then we should take the time to think whether we are making the right decision or not.

Another instance when a false dichotomy could lead us to a poor decision is when we trust the person who is presenting us with the false dichotomy. They may be a trusted friend or advisor and still mislead us unintentionally simply because they honestly believe that the false dichotomy is actually true and there are no other valid options. And sometimes, they may even be an expert that we refer to for a recommendation but who is biased for reasons which are not obvious to us. For example, they may get a special commission for selling a certain product or service, which then they may contrast with another option that is clearly inferior and we would never choose.

There are also situations when we either know or suspect better options could be available to us, but we decide not to look for those because we think they won't make much of a difference or just because we are lazy. This happens especially when the stakes are low and a poor decision won't affect us much or at all. For example, your partner may give the option of only two movies to watch. Both options are mildly interesting to you and you know that there are other movies available too, but decide to just pick one of the two instead of searching for another movie that both of you would enjoy more. The consequence of spending a couple of hours watching a very average movie is not that serious after all.

The opposite of the false dichotomy is **the paradox of choice**. Instead of having two distinct options to choose from, we face so many alternative options that it overwhelms us and we become unable to make up your mind. This happens all too often in our lives. For example, we might be buying an ice cream while on summer holiday and need to select only two or three flavors from their massive selection. Or, we might be trying to buy something on Amazon, maybe a new smart phone or a laptop, and the options seem endless.

In these situations, our agony of making a decision can last from a few minutes to several days or even weeks. We may never be satisfied that we made the right choice in the end, and we may wonder if another option would have been better for us. One very effective way to deal with an overwhelming number of options is to be fully aware and crystal clear of your needs or preferences in the first place. Then create a short list of the most important ones, and rank them one to five, in order of their priority and imagine your ideal option against these. By comparing this ideal option with all the available ones, you can very easily make the right choice. It will be either identical with your ideal choice or the one which is closest. If there are still two or more choices that are close to your ideal option, just take a short break or even sleep on it if necessary. Then review them again and make a choice once you are clear about which one is right. If you are still undecided, look at the exact differences between these remaining options and make a decision based on these. This approach should make it easy for you to make a good decision efficiently when faced with the paradox of choice. Additionally, asking other people for their opinion could also help in these situations, and you can always search for product reviews online. An unbiased expert opinion from someone with a good reputation and strong integrity can also be extremely useful when you face very complex decisions in unfamiliar areas.

False Dichotomy in the Real World

Back in the early 1970s, a young and hopeful actor went in for a casting call at a movie studio. He auditioned for a part, but quickly realized he was not right for it. On the way out, though, the young man mentioned a script for a pretty amazing story he had been working on. It was related to a real-life event, which was the fight between boxing great Muhammad Ali and tough underdog Chuck Wepner. The producers were intrigued, so they asked him to bring the script to them.

The young hopeful actor did just that. The producers read the script and they loved it. The young man wanted to play the main character, but the producers had no interest in that since the gentleman was an unknown with very little experience. They wanted a big-time actor with name recognition. For compensation, they offered him $360,000 to buy the script. Just imagine how much money this was back in the 1970s.

He was given two choices: Take the money or leave. Since the actor was quite impoverished and needed money, the obvious choice was taking the money. So, that's what he did, right? Well, actually not. He truly believed in his work and hoped that the story would become a huge hit, making him millions of dollars and a worldwide celebrity. He stuck to his guns and rejected their offer.

Eventually, the producers accepted his request and offered him $1 million to make the movie and have the starring role. This was his chance to make it big, and he certainly did. The story turned out to be one of the greatest franchises in cinematic history. This young actor's name was Sylvester Stallone, and the movie was Rocky. Luckily for us, Stallone did not fall for the false dichotomy presented to him. He knew there were other options. Obviously, he was right. No offense to any other actor, but can you imagine anyone else playing Rocky Balboa? [9]

Overcoming the False Dichotomy

False dichotomies can be very difficult to recognize at the moment they occur. When you are falsely given two choices and feel pressured to respond, you will get very anxious and this will reduce your ability to think properly. To help you recognize a false dichotomy claim, here are a couple more examples.

Science vs. Religion

Some people think that if you believe in one, then you cannot believe in the other. They think that accepting science means that you automatically reject religion or any religious experience.

In reality, belief in science and religion can coexist. One is not mutually exclusive of the other. For example, it is possible to believe in the Big Bang theory and also believe that God has created this event. There are numerous examples of great scientists who were also very religious people. For example, Isaac Newton (1643 - 1727) was a dissenting Protestant who was known to spend more time reading his bible than he actually spent on physics or math and Werner Heisenberg (1901 -

1976) who was one of the primary creators of the quantum mechanics and who was also a Lutheran with deep Christian convictions. What is probably even lesser known is that there are many scientists who start their careers as atheist but later in their lives start believing in God and become religious. Francis Collins (1950 - present), a geneticist who invented positional cloning and directed the National Human Genome Research Institute for 15 years, is one example of an atheist who has turned into a devout Christian during his career as an outstanding scientist.[10]

Saving vs. Spending Money

Some people have an all or nothing approach to money. They are so miserly with their money that they cut their expenses to the bare minimum so that they can save as much money as possible. Others, on the other hand, spend every penny they have and even borrow money or use credit to ensure to live as extravagantly as they can.

In reality, you should always try to live a balanced life by budgeting your finances carefully and avoiding either of these two extremes because either will have a very negative effect on your life in the long term. For example, if you are too extreme about saving money, you could miss a once in a lifetime chance to do something special with a loved one. Similarly, if you are too frivolous with your money, you may end up in massive debt and have a hard time trying to pay it back.

False dichotomies put you in an unfair situation where you feel heavily pressured to make a choice. Having to make a decision under pressure limits your ability to think about the other options there may be. Stop buying into the premise that things need to be either one way or the other. We don't always have to look to the extremes of a situation to get answers. The middle ground is often where the best answers are found.

When you accept a false dichotomy, you may be misled into making a poor choice. In most cases, you would make a completely different decision if you knew what other options you had. You must avoid the false dichotomies as much as possible. Here are a couple of things you can do.

TAKE YOUR TIME, **If You Can**

Most of us move so fast in life that we don't take our time to reflect on what is happening. If we paused more often, we would see things much more clearly. And if we stopped to think more carefully before any major decision, then our lives would be much better. We rarely do this though, and that is a problem. To overcome this issue, I encourage you to cultivate the habit of taking your time to think, even for the less important decisions in your life. Of course, you do not have to spend too much time thinking about the trivial things in your life. This would be a waste of time. As a guiding principle, when making a decision, the higher its impact, the more carefully you should consider that decision and the more time you should spend on clarifying your options.

SEARCH FOR HIDDEN **Or Less Known Options**

When presented with two options only, always wonder if other options are possible. Search for them on Google, YouTube, Quora, Facebook Groups, Yahoo Answers, etc. Ask your trusted friends and colleagues for their opinion. If the two options have been recommended by an expert, ask for a second or even a third expert opinion. Then determine whether any of the alternative options are indeed better than the initial ones. If time is an issue and you can't afford to spend any more time to look for and understand what other options are there, than just pick the best of the initial two. However, if there is no real emergency, give yourself a realistic deadline to find other options and look into them before making a final decision. Always be curious, but don't let your curiosity cause you miss a good opportunity for the sake of being curious.

Just keep in mind that not all the decisions that require you to choose between two options are false dichotomies or false dilemmas. In many cases, the two options you need to choose from are truly your best viable options out of many possible ones.

Stop and Think

When you are facing a choice between only two options, ask yourself:

- Is this really a black or white situation?
- Could this be a false dichotomy or a false dilemma instead?
- How much do I trust the information I have?
- Could other options be possible?
- Do I really have to make a decision now or can I delay it?
- Will I risk missing an opportunity if I take more time to decide? How likely is this risk? How big is the opportunity?
- How much time can I afford to spend searching for other options?

FIVE

Are Your Things Worth That Much?

"The value of a thing is always found by comparing it with other things."
Alfred Bishop Mason & John Joseph Lalor

Have you ever tried to sell something on eBay but were surprised to see that other people are selling the exact same thing in the exact same condition or similar for a much cheaper price than you expected? Most of us have been disappointed in this way at least once.

The **endowment effect** is an emotional bias that causes us to value things that we own much more than their real value simply because they are ours. Therefore, we place a higher value on the things that we are asked to give up than on similar things that we are asked to obtain. The endowment effect can be clearly seen with items that have an emotional or symbolic significance to us.[11]

American economist Richard Thaler was the first to begin studying the endowment effect systematically. He is also the one who coined the phrase 'endowment effect'. Through trying to determine what causes the endowment effect, Thaler came up with the idea of the having and not-having reference points. If you go from not having to having, it's a gain. If you go from having to not having, it's a loss. This may seem like an obvious formula, but it also has an underlying meaning. If a person loses $20 but then finds $20, the pain of losing the $20 will be greater than the joy of gaining it. Some studies have suggested that the feeling of loss is twice as powerful, psychologically, as the feeling of gain. This means that a loss is far more harmful to our psyche than an equivalent gain is beneficial to it. This psychological effect is called loss aversion.

The endowment effect affects our perception of value, even for the most inexpensive things that we own. However, it affects us the most when we are valuing our most expensive belongings, like a house or a car. When we want to sell our house, for example, especially after we have lived in it for a while, we tend to have very high expectations about its market value for no other good reason apart from the fact that it's ours. Unless we have a strong reason to sell the house within a time limit, we may even change our minds about selling it if we can't achieve a price close to our initial expectations. This may cause us to miss an opportunity to sell it at a good price, which we may not see again in a very long time if the property market takes a downturn while we are busy rejecting offers or soon after we put the sale on hold. The endowment effect can be even more pronounced, in this case, if we made significant improvements to the house which the buyers don't seem to appreciate much or at all.

The endowment effect can also affect new businesses rather significantly. Most entrepreneurs put in tremendous amounts of time of effort in creating and launching new products and services and then make the mistake of overpricing them. They have created something they care deeply about, it's theirs, and this powerful sense of ownership distorts their perception of value which causes them to overprice their products. While many of them are quick to realize that their initial prices are too high, not all these people are happy or willing to drop their prices to make their products more attractive. And this can be a very costly mistake that may lead to the failure of their new business. When you launch a new product or service, your priority should be to get sufficient market adoption as soon as possible and you should be ready to sacrifice your initial prices and profits to achieve this aim. Once you have strong sales volumes, you can increase your prices to maximize your profits. But you need those healthy sales volumes first, to confirm that there is a real market for your products. By focusing on sales volumes, you will also be able to achieve economies of scale, which will help you lower your costs in the long run, and to gain valuable insights about your customers and your business, which will then help you improve your products and profits even further.

Many businesses use the endowment effect to improve the sales of their products by offering free trials and no questions asked money-back guarantees for a limited time. This marketing tactic increases sales because once the customers use a product, they value it more than before because it's now in their possession and for this reason they are more likely to keep it rather than return it. This is a win-win situation, though, because as a customer you have the opportunity to try a product or service at no risk before buying it or to cancel the purchase within the money-back guarantee period. Of course, you need to be aware of the endowment effect and only keep those products and services that you truly need.

One consequence of the endowment effect is our tendency to accumulate things we don't really need. We either used these things once or just for a few times initially, or we never used them at all, and it's unlikely that we will ever do. And since we overvalue the things we own, we don't feel comfortable getting rid of anything we own, however unnecessary those things are. But the more things we accumulate, the harder it gets for us to keep them organized and we will end up surrounded by clutter. Unfortunately, excess clutter has a negative impact on our lives by making it difficult for us to find the things that we need when we need them, which slows us down, frustrates us and reduces our productivity.

Overvaluing the things we own can also prevent us from upgrading our gadgets and tools when this would benefit us. Many products are constantly getting upgraded over the years. The newer versions of these products become better and safer to use, and are more energy efficient too, because of newer materials, technology, and design. However, many of us are reluctant to upgrade our gadgets and tools because we think the ones that already own are more valuable than they really are. When we consider upgrading our old tech devices and we often get disappointed that we can't sell the ones we currently own for the price that we want. So, they end up belonging to us for much longer, which prevents us from enjoying and taking advantage of new gadgets and tools that are modern and efficient.

The opposite of the endowment effect is the **reversed endowment effect**, which means not valuing the things you own because you don't want them. For example, you may own an old chair, or an old painting, or any other old object that could get you thousands of dollars at an auction if you knew their true value. But you don't care about them at all because they don't look useful or appealing to you. There are countless stories of people who owned precious objects which they thought they were nothing special. For example, Loren

Krytzer, a Californian man, had an old blanket which he inherited from his grandmother and which no one else in his family wanted. As it turned out, the old blanket was not an ordinary blanket. It was a Navajo blanket, which was worth $1.5 million. Loren realized his blanket was immensely valuable in 2011, while watching an episode of Antiques Roadshow in which he saw an almost identical one which was valued at around half a million dollars.[12]

Even the most trivial things which you own may in fact be desirable to other people who would be willing to pay you more money that you would ever think possible. After all, who would think anyone would buy a broken laser pointer from an unknown seller on an unknown auction website? Well, Mark Fraser, a Canadian, bought it from Pierre Omidyar on eBay in 1995 and it was the first item ever bought on eBay. As they say, one man's trash is another man's treasure.

The Endowment Effect in the Real World

Lee Iacocca was a great businessman in the automotive industry, and many people speak of him in the same breath as someone like Henry Ford. Iacocca was the former CEO of Chrysler, and back in the 1980s, he had a brilliant idea that most people around him thought was insane. His plan was to start offering a 30-day money-back guarantee to all individuals who bought a car. If they weren't satisfied, they could just return the car within the grace period, with no questions asked.

The first thought that came to so many people's minds was that the buyers would drive around for 29 days and then return the car on the 30th day for no reason. This was a legitimate concern, and most of the people around Mr. Iacocca were not thrilled about this plan. However, Iacocca understood the endowment effect. His thought was that once people owned the car and had it in their possession, they would not be able to part with it. In addition, the 30-day money-back guarantee would make people less anxious about buying a car in the first place.

To the surprise of many, except for Mr. Iacocca, the marketing plan worked superbly. Car sales increased and less than two-tenths of one percent were returned. In effect, the new owners of the cars began creating new memories with them. They no longer had any intention of bringing the car back. Lee Iacocca was really considered a genius after this.[13]

From a business perspective, this is a beneficial example of the endowment effect. From the customer's standpoint, all I can say is, buyer beware! The endowment effect, or variations of it, is used by many salespeople in all industries. As a consumer, you must be aware of when you actually need something, rather than being coerced into buying something.

Overcoming the Endowment Effect

In general, we are not very good at putting the right price on our belongings. We overvalue the things we own and care about and undervalue the things that we own but don't care about. Here are some steps you can take to overcome the endowment effect.

EXPECT **Most Things To Lose Their Value In Time**

The accountants of this world know that most of the assets a company owns, with very few exceptions, such as land and buildings, lose their value in time. They call this depreciation. They also know that different things lose their value at different rates, which they try to estimate. These estimates are never perfectly accurate, but they are useful for accounting purposes. For this reason, when an asset is sold to another company, its actual selling price will most likely be different from its estimated value, also known as book value. In order to reduce the impact of the endowment effect on our lives, we should follow the accountants' example. We should always expect the things we own to lose value over time, we should always expect different things to lose their value at different speeds, and we should always expect to be wrong about the exact price we can sell them for.

ALWAYS FIND Out The True Market Value Of The Things You Want To Sell

Because the endowment effect can mislead us into believing that the things that we own are much more valuable than they truly are, the most likely outcome is that no one else will share our opinion and we will never find a buyer for our overpriced things. Whether these are brand new goods or used, or even services that we provide, we should always find out their true market value. We should always do our own price research in order to know their true and objective value and avoid being disappointed or miss opportunities to sell them. For our price research, we can ask other sellers or buyers of identical or similar items or check out prices online. It is important that from our price research we know both the minimum and the maximum price people normally pay when buying from other places, and also what factors are driving the price up and down and whether we can influence those or not. Armed with this information, we should be able to determine a realistic market price for our goods or services.

. . .

REMOVE **The Clutter From Your Home**

Removing the clutter from your home or office could also help. One way to do this is to place all the things you haven't used in a while and no longer need into a box and seal it. On the box write an expiration date that is about three to six months away and set up a reminder in your smart phone or make a note about it in your calendar. Do not open the box unless you absolutely need something from it. If you need something from it, don't place that item back after using it. Then, on the expiration date, just sell the content of that box on eBay or on a specialized website where you can get the best price for those items.

You may not get rid of the endowment effect completely, but you can definitely minimize its influence over you if you take these steps.

Stop and Think

When trying to sell a product or a service that you own, ask yourself:

- Am I overpricing my product or service just because it's mine?
- Why would anyone pay the price I am asking for? Is there anything unique about it? Is it scarce?
- What is the current price for this product or service, or for similar ones?
- Where can I get a realistic valuation for it?
- Will I risk missing a window of opportunity if I overprice this product or service?

SIX

Blinded by A Good Impression

"There is nothing so stupid as an educated man, if you get him off the thing he was educated in."
Will Rogers

Have you ever seen a successful business person venture into politics only to disappoint the vast majority of people who initially trusted him or her? I am sure that we have all seen someone like this.

A **halo effect** is a cognitive bias that causes our positive impressions of a person in one area to positively influence our opinion or feelings about them in other areas too. Besides individuals, the halo effect can also influence our opinions about products, services, brands, companies or any other type of organizations.[14]

The halo effect was first observed and reported in the early 1900s. The term was coined by the psychologist, Edward Thorndike. He performed an experiment with military commanding officers. He asked these officers to evaluate their subordinates based on a few characteristics. He wanted to see if the perception of excellence or deficiency in one characteristic led to the same perception about other characteristics. Thorndike found that high ratings in a specific quality resulted in high ratings for other qualities. For example, a subordinate who was taller and more attractive was also rated as more intelligent, despite there being no evidence to support this. Several other studies throughout the years have shown similar results.

The perception of a positive personal trait or feature can influence our perception of all the other aspects of a person or a thing. When we allow this to happen, we are unfairly judging people or things without really getting to know them.

Those who are well aware of the halo effect and make an effort to overcome it will get to know people for who they really are. On the other hand, people who are not aware of the halo effect or ignore it are often fooled into misjudging others, only to be disappointed later.

One common manifestation of the halo effect is how some celebrities influence our lives. In most areas of their lives, most celebrities are no better than ordinary people, yet we tend to think that if they excel in one thing, they must excel in everything. Some people even worship some celebrities and try to imitate them to a certain extent. We also use some celebrities for inspiration or guidance about our own beliefs. For example, a famous actress that we are very fond of can influence our views on politics or lifestyle choices, not because they are an expert in those areas but because we like her for her acting career.

This powerful influence that celebrities have on us has been used successfully for decades by the advertising industry to promote a wide variety of brands and products. We are all very well familiar with this type of ads featuring a famous person sporting a happy smile while using a product and telling us how great it is, but have you ever wondered how much money the top celebrities get for endorsing consumer products? Here are some examples: George Clooney was paid $40 million to endorse Nespresso, Serena Williams was paid $55 million to endorse Nike, Beyonce was paid $50 million to endorse Pepsi, and Sofia Vergara was paid $94.5 million to endorse a number of brands, including Pepsi, Quaker Oats, Head & Shoulders and CoverGirl.[15] Well, if you want to make some easy money, all you have to do is to become a top celebrity and then sign a lucrative endorsement deal with a top brand. There is no better way.

The halo effect can have a significant influence on people's careers, too. An employer may overlook an employee's lack of skills when hiring or promoting them if an employee is well liked for their personality or looks. In the food-service industry, servers who were considered more attractive earned $1,200 more per year on average. A study conducted in 2005 had potential employers look at pictures of potential employees. The study determined that the employers were ready to give the more attractive people an average of 10.5% higher salaries. Psychologists call the income gap between attractive and unattractive people the beauty premium.

Can the halo effect affect our personal lives too? Well, yes, quite significantly, actually. The halo effect may cause us to make friends with people based on one or two salient qualities that we like. We may, for instance, be automatically attracted to good-looking or charming people and expect them to somehow be good friends to us. But if these people are not truly compatible with us, we will end up in negative relationships with these people. By focusing only on their very few qualities and ignoring all their faults, we risk wasting our time and energy on people that do not make us happy or add value to our lives. Similarly, ignoring otherwise good people because there is something about them that we don't like or understand leads us to missing out on positive, interesting relationships that could enhance our lives.

One of the most traumatizing ways in which the halo effect can affect our lives is when we fall in love with a narcissist. A narcissist is characterized by an enormous ego, complete lack of empathy, and selfish behavior. Additionally, they are secretive, they lie, they cheat on their partners; they are oversensitive to criticism, however small, they overreact, they throw tantrums, even in public places, and it's impossible to have a rational discussion with them when they upset you. Their most shocking behavior is gaslighting. Gaslighting is trying to make someone question their memories and reality by lying to them or manipulating them. Narcissists are cold and calculated people users who don't truly care about other people's feelings. They are usually very attractive and very good at initiating new relationships. Getting involved with a narcissist can feel amazing at first because of their beauty and also because they tend to overwhelm you with their attention. But your dream will sooner or later turn into a nightmare, and breaking free from their influence could be extremely difficult and may require help from an experienced therapist.

Who you surround yourself with determines the direction of your life, at least to a certain extent. The people that you look to for guidance and advice should be worthy of your trust. This is why controlling the halo effect should be a key concern for you. When you look beyond the most dominant impression and truly get to know a person, you can form a far more objective view of their character and avoid being misled and making poor decisions in your life.

A more subtle way in which the halo effect influences our lives is through first impressions. When we meet someone for the very first time, if they make a positive first impression on us, we will most likely have a positive attitude towards that person and be receptive to everything they say during the meeting. Additionally, the halo effect will also cause us to focus on the positives and ignore the negatives. If, however, they make a negative first impression on us, we will most likely have a negative attitude towards that person and unwilling to listen to them. Additionally, the negative halo effect will cause us to focus on the negatives and ignore the positives during our interaction with the other person.

The negative halo effect is known as **the horn effect**. The horn effect means that you associate a single negative experience with a person, a product, or a service with everything else about them. It's very easy for us to get very emotional and become very judgmental and vengeful in the heat of the moment when we feel we were treated unfairly or in a very unhelpful or non-empathic way. Despite this, it's in our best interest to be as objective and fair as possible and to achieve this we need to re-assess any bad situation when we are calm and can clearly understand our options and the best way forward.

Halo Effect in the Real World

For those of you who are professional wrestling fans, you have probably heard the name Vince McMahon. He has been the largest wrestling promoter since the 1980s, and by the early 2000s, he had no real competition. Mr. McMahon took the momentum from his success with World Wrestling Entertainment and used it to start an extreme football league, known as the XFL.

This was expected to be a huge success, and many investors jumped on board to get their share of the pie. Even a large television network, NBC, invested millions of their own money to make it a joint venture. People assumed that Vince McMahon had the Midas touch at this point because of his extreme success in the wrestling world. The XFL was being billed as more extreme than other football leagues, and a lot of promotion and hype occurred before the initial game.

Unfortunately, the idea turned out to be a flop. The first game received a lot of interest. People were curious and excited about what they would see. However, the viewership declined steadily as people lost interest, and by the end of the first season, the league was at death's door. A common complaint people had was that they saw too much pro wrestling mixed into it. While WWE was extremely popular, sports fans did not want to see it while watching football.

The XFL did not get renewed for a second season. Both Vince McMahon and NBC lost millions of dollars on this joint venture, even though it was expected to be a huge success. It is estimated that about 70 million dollars was lost.[16]

Overcoming the Halo Effect

Now that we understand how the halo effect can influence us, here are some steps that could help you avoid this cognitive bias.

BE Conscious Of Your Judgments

To prevent the halo effect from affecting you, you must acknowledge your inclination to judge people too quickly or based on insufficient information. Try to look beyond your initial opinion about them. If your opinion about someone is based on how attractive they are or based solely on some other well-known quality or theirs, take a step back. Take your time to learn all the relevant information about this person first, then you should be able to form a fair opinion about them. Learning to make well informed and fair judgments about people without being influenced by the halo effect will help you in the long term by preventing you from trusting the wrong people for the wrong reasons. Use this approach to form fair opinions about other things in your life too, such as products and services, brands and organizations, and so on.

QUESTION **Your First Impression**

Because we often judge people based on our initial impressions about them and a tiny amount of information, it's important to suspend our judgment when we meet someone new until we get to know them better. Someone who seems nice and smart initially may turn out to be nasty and narrow minded later, and someone who seems nasty and difficult at first may actually be nice and easy to deal with once we know them better. Always avoid rushing to form a firm opinion about people and things based on your first impressions.

TRUST **Your Intuition**

Trust your intuition or gut feelings. If you have a strong negative feeling about somebody when you first meet them, take into account this feeling, don't ignore it. Most likely, your subconscious mind has picked up subtle signals from the other person and tries to alert you that something is not right. It could be something about their body language or voice that alerts your subconscious mind that something is wrong. This could be your survival instinct kicking in. Just be alert and, if you feel anxious, end the meeting as soon as possible. You can re-schedule it if you want to make sure that you are not making a mistake. After all, your intuition could sometimes be wrong.

Stop and Think

When someone who is an expert in one field ventures into a new field, or a company launches products or services which are different from what they are usually known for, ask yourself:

- Does this make any sense at all?
- Have other people or companies been successful in similar scenarios?
- Can this person or company really be successful with this new endeavor in the long run?
- How do they describe their decision to use their position to influence others?
- Are you allowing yourself to be influenced by someone's opinion without knowing the actual facts behind the issue or topic?
- Am I judging this person based on superficial aspects such as looks, income or fame?
- Do I have an opportunity to learn more about this person or thing before I decide if their opinion is valuable to me?

SEVEN

False Causes in Disguise

"There is no more dangerous error than confounding consequence with cause."
Friedrich Nietzsche

Have you ever been accused of doing something wrong that you haven't done? Either by your parents, or by your friends or colleagues, or someone else. Let's say something valuable disappeared, and they thought you took it. The accusation took you by surprise, and most likely you didn't even know how to react. Much to your disbelieve, they were absolutely convinced of your wrongdoing because you were the only person whom they had seen in that area just before realizing something was missing. But later they had to apologize to you because they found the real culprit. I am sure that something similar happened to most of us, or that at least we know someone who has been in this situation. The two events, the disappearance of the valuable object and your presence, were correlated in the eyes of others because they happened at the same time, but someone else took the object, not you.

A **false cause fallacy** happens when we don't know the true cause of an event, and we wrongly assume or were led to believe that one of two events occurring together or in sequence has caused the other. There are two variations of this fallacy.

A **questionable-cause fallacy** happens when two events occurring together make us believe that one has caused the other. In other words, it happens when we assume that there is an established cause-and-effect relationship between them. This fallacy is often defined by the Latin phrase *cum hoc ergo propter hoc* ("with this, therefore because of this").

A **false causality fallacy** happens when two events occurring one after the other make us believe that the first event has caused the second. In this case, there is a very clear sequence of events, but the two events may not even be related.[17] This fallacy is described in Latin as *post hoc ergo propter hoc* ("after this, therefore because of this").

Here is a scenario that illustrates a questionable-cause fallacy. Picture a store near a beach that sells various things throughout the year. Every year, the sales of ice cream and sunglasses skyrocket in July and August, then drop in September. The sales of ice cream and sunglasses are clearly correlated, but we know that there is no causation. The actual cause is the hot and sunny days in July and August. The increased sales of sunglasses have nothing to do with the increased sales of ice cream. However, if you offered a discount on sunglasses with each purchase of an ice cream, there would be a cause-and-effect relationship between the increased sales of ice cream and the increased sales of sunglasses.

The truth is, every event in the world is caused by something, but the causes are not always obvious and sometimes what we see as the obvious cause is not the true cause at all. In many cases, there are several potential variables at play, which makes it difficult for us to understand the true cause. The more that is unknown about a situation, the more theories there will be. A lack of complete and accurate information will make people reach the wrong conclusions about the true cause or causes.

If you think the false cause fallacy affects other people and remote events that you only learn about from the internet or TV and it's not likely to affect you, think again. In the US alone, every year about 12 million people are misdiagnosed by medical doctors. That is 1 in 5, or 20% of the total adult patients. The most commonly misdiagnosed illnesses include cancer, celiac disease, stroke, lupus, heart attack, and blood clot in the lungs.[18] Why does this happen though? After all, with so much advanced technology these days available to assist the doctors in making accurate diagnoses, you wouldn't expect such a high number of misdiagnosed patients. Unfortunately, the doctors don't always have access to the right equipment and devices for accurate diagnosis, and some doctors are so busy that they only have limited time to see their patients or have to deal with constant interruptions. The patients can also play a role in getting misdiagnosed by not mentioning all their symptoms or relevant details about their medical history.

Besides medicine, there are many other fields where misdiagnosing problems can happen frequently. Any complex system that malfunctions can be difficult to diagnose correctly. In fact, the more complex the system, the harder it is to diagnose it accurately. For instance, your PC can slow down or become very noisy for many reasons, your car can also start consuming too much gas for many reasons, or a space rocket can explode at launch for a countless number reasons, and in all these cases we could very easily fail to determine the root cause of the problem due to the sheer complexity of these systems and also due to the subtle interactions between their components.

Sadly, the false cause fallacy can destroy innocent people's lives. This happens when innocent people are sent to prison for criminal acts they haven't committed. Malcolm Alexander is one of these people. He was arrested for rape based on uncertain identification from the victim and then convicted to life without parole in a trial that last one day. He was only 21 years old. In 2018, after being incarcerated for almost 38 years, Malcolm was finally released from Louisiana's Angola prison based on DNA testing sought by the Innocence Project.[19] The Innocence Project, an organization that exonerates people who have been wrongfully convicted of crimes in the United States, has estimated that between 2.3 percent and 5 percent of all US prisoners are in fact innocent. That means that as many as 120,000 people in the US have been sent to prison for wrongful convictions.[20]

Many people have been wrongfully accused of things they had nothing to do with. They are many innocent victims in our society. People have lost their jobs, homes, families, livelihoods, freedoms, and even lives because people assumed they were the cause of something. There are countless people who were sent to prison simply because they were in the wrong place at the wrong time.

The similarities between causation and correlation can be used to persuade, dissuade, or manipulate. For example, the media and those in power can divert attention away from true culprits and victims of a situation. They can do this by showing only the parts of the story that support one view of the event.

You must recognize when someone is trying to manipulate you in this manner. You must also recognize when you mistakenly assume a causal relationship, simply based on correlation. There can be many different reasons why a particular event happens, and you cannot simply assume the simplest answer is correct.

There is variation of the false cause fallacy called the **fundamental attribution error,** which leads us to overemphasize personal factors and either ignore or under-estimate the context, i.e. situational factors, when explaining people's behavior.

The fundamental attribution error is responsible for many hiring mistakes in business. Many people have very impressive resumes, filled with achievements often while working for well-known companies, but although these people appear to have delivered those impressive results or at least to have played an instrumental role in delivering them, they actually haven't done anything beyond ordinary. They just happened to be in the right place at the right time, did a very average job, while other people in their company were in fact responsible for those impressive results.

Let's take an example from sales. Let's assume that a new sales director has been headhunted to lead the sales team of an established company. He comes from a much more successful company in the same industry and has delivered a very impressive performance in the past couple of years. To motivate him to change companies, his new company offered him a premium salary package, which was 50% better than what he made before. However, 6 months into the new job, the sales are not improving in line with the initial expectations and the new sales director doesn't seem to make any difference at all. What can possibly explain his disappointing performance? Several things actually, including a change in his personal life, but a very common scenario that can explain his lackluster performance is a switch from selling top products that essentially sold themselves because the customers were lining up to buy them, to selling average products are very similar to several others in the market and that the customers don't feel compelled to buy, unless persuaded by a talented salesperson. You don't need to be a highly skilled salesperson to sell a top product, which is in high demand, but you do need to be a highly skilled salesperson to sell an average product in a highly competitive market. By failing to understand the true reason for his apparent success with his previous company, the people who decided to hire this sales director have committed the fundamental attribution error.

When making assumptions about a causal relationship, you can be wrong about the real cause, but you can also fail to understand the **unintended consequences** or side effects of a known cause or of a solution to fix a problem. In many instances, a solution for a problem can indeed cause unexpected side consequences in addition to solving the actual problem. These consequences can be negative, positive, or neutral, and they can also vary in terms of their magnitude and be either significant or insignificant. Take the Covid-19 pandemic as an example. The UK government, like many other governments across the globe, has rushed to implement a nationwide lockdown in the fight against the virus. As a result of it, the UK's economy took a severe blow and its gross domestic product (GDP) fell by a record 20.4% in the second quarter of 2020 compared to the first quarter of the same year.[21] This was an unintended consequence of epic proportions. Will the UK government make the exact same decision in similar circumstances in the future? Of course not. The UK government has already confirmed that it won't impose any further nationwide lockdowns that could cripple the country's already battered economy; it will only impose localized ones.

But can you ever trust these people? I am not sure you can, to be honest. Anyway, it is not always easy to predict the magnitude or even the existence of an unintended consequence when trying a new solution, but we should always keep our eyes open and take very rapid action before any unintended consequence spirals out of control.

False Cause Fallacy in the Real World

There have been many terrific movies made throughout history, and it can be hard to say exactly what made the movie great. Sometimes, it is the acting, while other times it can be production value, the storyline, special effects, or a combination of everything. In regard to actors, there are a select few who are phenomenal, to the point where they can act in anything and give a stellar performance. In other instances, an actor or actress may have had one or two hits, but everything else flopped.

This leads me to believe that they were not talented enough actors, and they did not truly have the magic that was once perceived. Basically, actors and actresses are often thought to have made a movie successful. However, there are other factors that actually made them irrelevant. If other performers had filled the role, there would not have been much of a difference. The individual actors and actresses did not make the movie great; they just happened to be in a great movie.

An example of this is actor Robert Pattinson from the *Twilight* saga. This movie series was a great hit and truly put Pattinson on the map. Many people praised his performance, and he was heralded as a great actor. He was given additional roles based on the success of this movie. Unfortunately, Pattinson's performances fell short on any projects after the *Twilight* series. This made several movie experts realize that Pattinson was not the cause of *Twilight*'s success, he just happened to be in a movie that had a great storyline, production value, and supporting cast.

While I am not saying Robert Pattinson is not talented, he is not as significant in the acting world as the blockbuster *Twilight* would lead you to believe. It's a reasonable argument to make that other actors could have filled the role and the movies would have been just as good. Of course, we will never know for sure. Some people out there will probably disagree with this, but that's okay because we all have an opinion. Pattinson found little success after his role as a vampire. For example, the movie *Water for Elephants* did not do well at the box office, and in 2019, critics felt that he did not have the star power to bring in fans for his movie, *Waiting for the Barbarians*.[22]

Overcoming the False Cause Fallacy

It is easy for people to start believing that two events impact each other if they seem associated closely. However, to keep yourself from jumping to conclusions, you must think about the other variables involved. Two events cannot simply be assumed to impact each other because they are closely related in some way.

To overcome the false causation fallacy, always live with the belief that there is more to a situation than meets the eye. There is often more than one possible cause that can explain an effect, so you must seek to understand the whole picture and look for other possible causes beyond the most apparent one before drawing any conclusions.

Here are some additional actions you can take to overcome the false cause fallacy.

. . .

REMEMBER How Easy It Is to Jump to the Wrong Conclusion

First impressions are often wrong. Recall past incidents and reflect on the times where you jumped to the wrong conclusion based on misinformation or oversimplified information. Use these moments to remind yourself that there may be more to the story.

KEEP Your Emotions At Bay

Avoid acting purely on emotions and take your time to come to a conclusion. False causal relationships often occur because people are too emotional and impatient to discover the whole truth. Learn to slow down. Taking a long walk can help you calm down and reorganize your thoughts. Taking deep breaths is also an effective way to calm your nerves. If these two methods don't work, distance yourself from the situation for a while, a few hours at least, by focusing on something else. Another effective way to keep your emotions at bay is to ask people who can help you for their advice. Speaking to someone can help you get a better understanding of the situation you are facing, even if they don't know what to say or how to help you. Sometimes, a five-minute chat with a friend is all you need to calm down and act rationally.

ALWAYS MAKE Sure That You Understand The Context

Make an effort to see the whole picture, to get the entire perspective. This will help you better understand people and their motives. For example, instead of assuming that a person treats people poorly because they are a jerk or have poor people skills, ask yourself what exactly makes them behave this way. Do they always behave this way or just in certain circumstances or with certain people? This is not meant to excuse their behavior, but to enable you to understand if there is a context for the behavior.

VALIDATE **The Causal Effect By Invalidating The Other Likely Causes**

When stakes are high, always ask yourself what other causes could explain what you see and then check if there is any evidence to support any of these other potential causes. If there is no proof for an alternative explanation, then chances are that what appears to be the cause is indeed the true cause. As Arthur Conan Doyle said, "Once you eliminate the impossible, whatever remains, no matter how improbable, must be the truth."

USE **The 5 Whys Technique To Determine The Root Cause Of Any Problem**

The 5 Whys technique is a series of questions that will help you analyze a problem to determine its root cause. Five is just a guideline. The actual number of questions doesn't need to be exactly five. Just ask as many why questions as necessary. Here is a simple example of how it works. Let's assume that someone has been frequently late for their online meetings recently. Why are they late? Because they can't get their laptop to connect to the meeting on time. Why? Because they get confused about how to join the meeting. Why do they get confused? Because different meetings with different people require using different apps and they don't always know what steps to follow to join the current meeting and whether or not they need to download any additional software to join the meeting. Why don't they always know the steps to follow to join the meeting? Because they assume joining the meeting is straightforward and don't check if this is true beforehand. As you can see from this example, the root cause of being frequently late is assuming that joining the online meetings is always straightforward and not checking if their assumption is correct before their meetings to avoid being late. Knowing this, this person needs to test connecting to the online meetings ahead of time, at least one hour before the start, to make sure they know the exact steps to connect and to have the chance to fix any technical issues that could prevent them from joining the meeting.

Stop and Think

When two factors, let's call them A and B, are correlated, ask yourself?

- How do I know for sure that A has been caused by B? What proof do I have?
- What if B has been caused by A instead? Is there any proof for this?
- Is it possible that both A and B have been caused by a hidden factor C?
- Is it possible that there is no cause-and-effect relationship between A and B?

EIGHT

The Downside of Playing Safe

"Familiarity reduces the greatness of things."
Seneca the Younger

Have you ever booked a hotel simply because you were very familiar with that specific hotel brand? Let's take Hilton, as an example. You stayed at other Hilton hotels before and always had a pleasant experience. However, later you learned that there were better options available to you when you were booking your stay, but you quickly discarded them without much thought. And then, to your surprise, you found out from other people that you could have stayed in a nicer hotel with better amenities and in a better location for a lower price, but this hotel was completely unknown to you. You made your choice based on your familiarity with the Hilton brand and missed a better choice as a result.

Familiarity bias causes us to choose familiar options (products, services, people) over unfamiliar ones when we have the opportunity to do so. We do this in order to avoid the risks and stress associated with trying something different.

Most people in this world live their lives in ways which are familiar to them in spite of having options for a better life or at least for better life experiences. They would rather keep on the path they know than venture out and try something new, even when they have nothing to lose.

Take our social circles as an example. Most of us spend our time in the company of the same people, whether friends, colleagues or family. We tend to isolate ourselves from the outside world and spend our time with people who are like-minded. However, spending time only with those people who are familiar to us can limit our lives and minds. And even worse, the familiarity bias can lead us to be around people who bring us down.

If your inner circle is holding you back, then it may be time to change who you keep inside of it. As Jim Rhon famously said, we are the average of the five people we spend the most time with. While these five people are our inner circle and our future is influenced by them, this number is not set in stone. It will be slightly different for each of us and it will also change as we move through our lives because people change, circumstances change, and our priorities change as well.

Another very common way in which the familiarity bias influences our lives is when we decide to buy a new product or service. Apple, Amazon, Sony, Samsung, Microsoft, Nike, Hilton, Gillette, Coca-cola, Starbucks, McDonald's. What do all these names have in common? They are all familiar brand names. When buying something and we have the option of choosing between a known and reputable brand and an unknown brand, the familiarity bias makes favor of the known brand, as in the Hilton example above. And some of us will rely on this one single criteria to decide what to buy without considering how good the other options are, which may in fact work better for us, like in the Hilton example.

The commercial brands that we are familiar with have their merits, for sure, and they do live up to their reputation in most cases, but not always. And the price premium that we pay for them compared to price we would pay for the cheaper alternatives is also very often justified, but not always. Unless a product or service is truly unique and perfect for our needs, we should always look beyond our familiarity with the brand when deciding what's best for us.

These days, the internet makes it easier for us than ever before to make an informed buying decision but it's still time-consuming to read product reviews or watch them on YouTube and this effort could quickly expand out of control and overwhelm us if we are considering too many options or the decision is too complicated and difficult to make.

The current speed of product innovation is unprecedented in the human history. New products are launched to market every day, and many of them are indeed superior to the existing ones intended to gain market share and disrupt the market. But these new and innovative products are most often created by start-ups that no one knows about and because of this most potential buyers are reluctant to buy them. After all, these people's familiarity with these new products and start-ups making them is zero. And this zero usually cancels all the evidence that shows how much better these new products are.

Unfortunately, we miss countless of opportunities to benefit from better products and services due to our familiarity biases and because we are too lazy to weigh our options properly.

In the investment world, the familiarity bias occurs when investors fail to diversify their investments and continue investing in the same company or familiar companies, even after getting lower than expected results for a long time. They end up losing their money on something they know rather than investing in the potential of something they don't know.

There are three main familiarity biases that affect the investment world and that you need to be aware of as a new investor, according to Dr. Kent Baker, a Professor of Finance at American University.[23]

- Bias toward your home country, so you only buy investments in companies that are nationally or locally owned
- Bias toward the company you work for, so you only buy stock in that company or other companies owned by the same parent group
- Bias toward a company that you like yourself, so you buy stocks in products and companies that you buy products or services from, or that you like for other reasons, such as their environmental policies

Many investors are reluctant to even consider investing in companies which they are not familiar with regardless of the current trends or of what the industry experts predict for the future. For this reason, these investors fail to diversify their portfolios, which then results in inferior or poor performance. Many opportunities are lost when you are afraid of taking risks, which, in the world of finance, you can always hedge against in order to limit any potential loses.

The cause of familiarity bias is essentially the need for security. We dislike feeling anxious, whether it is physically, emotionally, or mentally. We want to live comfortable lives and avoid doing anything that could disrupt our comfort. We also like to be in control of our lives, and the more familiarity we have in our lives, the more we feel in control.

The opposite of the familiarity bias is **the novelty bias**. This means always wanting to try new things. In addition to a high appetite for novelty, you need to have a few more things if you want to try new things in a smart way rather than a foolish way. You need to have access, the right resources, the right skills, sufficient energy, and risk management.

Access means simply being able to access the new experience that you are seeking. For example, if you want to take a space flight on a Virgin Galactic spacecraft, you need to be patient because it will only start its commercial operations in 2021 and there is also a long waiting list of eager people. This means that you won't have access to this experience for a few years. And if you want to visit the rings of Saturn, your access to this life experience is blocked for the foreseeable future. Having the right resources means mostly having the money and time to afford the new experience. Although a space flight on a Virgin Galactic spacecraft doesn't require a significant time commitment, not many people can afford to pay $250,000 for a 90 minute flight in space.[24]

Although trying something new doesn't always require any new skills, having the right skills is sometimes needed before you can enjoy a new experience. Skiing down on the most amazing mountains in the Austrian Alps, for example, won't be too enjoyable or safe if you can barely ski. So, learning to ski competently is a must for anyone who wants to enjoy this beautiful sport and make the most of the beautiful alpine scenery and its fresh air. Regardless of what type of new activity you are engaged in, your brain consumes more energy than usual when faced with novelty as it tries to make sense of the new information and tries to fit it within your existing knowledge. The higher the novelty level, the more energy you need to cope with your new experience. That's why if you are new to skiing, you are exhausted at the end of a day of skiing not as much from the physical effort as from the mental effort necessary to learn a very complex skills. Your more experienced friends will always have significantly more energy at the end of a skiing day than you as a novice skier. Compared to you, they are not learning anything new but are just using their well-honed skills and fully enjoy the whole skiing experience.

Finally, risk management is paramount when you are trying a new experience. Always be cautious, always listen to your gut feeling when you are in a new situation, and always live by the "better safe than sorry" words of wisdom. This means, if you sense that something is wrong or not quite right, be ready to get out of that situation either immediately or as soon as possible. Whenever you want to try something new, a business, a sport, or just to visit a new place, always assess the risks involved and be prepared to deal with those risks in the most effective way, including calling the whole thing off to protect yourself.

Familiarity Bias in the Real World

Kodak is a name that is synonymous with photography. At least, it once was. Even though the company is still around, it has much less influence than it once had. Kodak was actually at the forefront of technology when it invented the first digital camera in 1975. This innovation should have launched them into the stratosphere, based on where we are now in regard to the digital world. Unfortunately, the higher-ups in Kodak did not recognize the potential, as they were too shortsighted. Back then, the company had a lucrative film business and did not want to hurt or ignore this area of their organization, which they thought would be cannibalized by the new digital technology. They figured their marketing campaigns would offset and eventually eliminate any need for digital products. After all, Kodak's marketing executives had done a great job at weaving the brand into the fabric of American culture. Unfortunately, these executives underestimated the power of digital. As a result, they continued on their usual track of focusing and improving on their film business. Their past success made them resistant to any type of major change.

In the meantime, their competitors, like Sony and Canon, jumped on digital cameras and charged forward with them. They embraced the new technology while Kodak continued with what was familiar to them.

Eventually, Kodak realized the error of its ways when its main competitors were surpassing them in the marketplace. When they tried to jump onto the digital train, it was far too late, as Sony and Canon were far ahead in digital technology by this point. Unfortunately, Kodak could never catch up and declared bankruptcy in 2012. They reemerged in 2013, but their presence is not nearly what it was in decades past.

Kodak's fatal error was that it did not adapt to the requirements of the market. They simply felt they could force-feed their old-school products down people's throats with amazing marketing plans. Kodak learned the hard way that smart marketing means providing products and services that the public needs and demands. Therefore, resistance to change and staying with what is familiar can become a death sentence to any business.

Imagine how much farther along Kodak would be if it followed the momentum of their 1975 digital innovation.

Unfortunately, their stubbornness caused them to miss out on an amazing opportunity.[25]

Overcoming Familiarity Bias

In order to overcome the familiarity bias and avoid its limiting effects, you must make a mental effort to step outside your comfort zone, to weigh your options properly and make the right decisions. There is no way around this. We all have habits which we have developed over time, whether intentionally or unintentionally. Habits take a while to develop, yet it is very easy to fall into a routine that does not serve you well. Therefore, the key is to focus on good habits and develop those every day. Think of busting the familiarity bias as a good habit to develop. Since our brains are wired to take the path of least resistance, we can change the wiring to start getting out of our comfort zones. We do this by consciously and constantly pushing the boundaries.

RELAX, To See More Options

Humans tend to become narrow minded and ultra focused when involved in a stressful situation. While this is amazing for becoming productive, you also lose your creative abilities. Our ability to think becomes limited. In these times, we automatically revert back to what is familiar to us. Psychologist Barbara Frederickson discovered through her research that play and happiness lead to a higher capacity for understanding alternatives. This means we are more likely to venture out into the unknown when we are happy and not overly stressed.

Even in times of great distress, if we can find some levity, we can come up with improved solutions. This is why children are great at exploring and finding new things. They love to play and find happiness, which means they have very little fear of the unknown. Their entire lives revolve around learning what they don't know yet. As adults, we lose the ability to play and therefore our creativity is often lost too. So, we settle into familiar patterns. It makes our lives much easier, and most people love what is easy.

Therefore, in order to improve your chances of finding, or even seeing, the alternative options besides the familiar ones, and to overcome the familiarity bias, you must be in a more relaxed state to begin with. Otherwise, you will most likely overlook any alternative options regardless of how clear they are.

START **With Small Changes**

Cultivate the habit of trying new things, at least once in a while, by starting with small things that you buy regularly. If you always go to Starbucks for your coffee, try a different coffee shop for a change, or different type of coffee at Starbucks. You may discover a drink that you like more than your usual coffee. What do you have to lose, anyway? Few dollars if you don't like the change, but you also learn something new. Similarly, if you are fixated on a particular restaurant, force yourself to try a different one, from time to time, or buy a different starter or main course than your usual if you always get the same food and if this is easier than changing the restaurant. Trying new things in this manner will help you find better alternatives to the ones you are used to in some cases, and it will make your life more interesting and also give you something to talk about with your friends in all cases.

EVALUATE ALL **The Available Options Carefully**

When buying more expensive or complex products or services, you need to define the minimum criteria that the new product or service must meet for you to buy it. These can include features, price, warranty, brands, reviews, delivery time, etc. and they will help you identify your best option while removing the familiarity bias. Just make sure you don't limit the brands to those which are familiar to you, unless you have to. If you want to buy a product from reputable brand, but similar products from less-known brands are available too, you should not automatically discard those. You should at least check the best products from those less-known brands on Amazon to get an understanding on how they compare with the ones from the well-known brands. You will be surprised to see that sometimes the best products in come from the less-known brands.

DIVERSIFY Your Investments

If you are new to investing and want to reduce the risk of losing money by investing in just one company or a handful of very similar ones, look for options to diversify your portfolio by investing in companies you are not familiar with. You do need to research these unfamiliar companies beforehand and have at least some basic understanding of their products and services, customers, industry trends and competitive landscape, and also their key financials in order to make informed investment decisions. Additional diversification strategies include investing in bonds, currencies, or commodities. Because these additional investments require more effort for additional research and analysis, most new investors won't take this path. However, if you are serious about investing, you should make an effort to overcome your familiarity bias and diversify your investments.

. . .

DON'T LET **The Imposter Syndrome Deter You**

As mentioned in chapter 1, the imposter syndrome is common among people who put themselves in unfamiliar situations, when starting new roles, new careers or new hobbies. Sometimes, the imposter syndrome can even last for few good years before disappearing. If you suffer from it, you have to remember that it is natural, that you are not the only one affected by it, and that it will eventually subside and disappear. Just focus on your strengths, monitor your progress, and don't let it deter you.

CHECK **Other People's Perspective**

It's always a good idea to ask people who can advise you for their opinion before buying something new or embarking on a novel experience. You can learn valuable information, avoid rookie mistakes, get practical help and even get introduced to other people who can help you further.

Stop and Think

When you are faced with situations that are familiar to you and your natural instinct is to do what you've always done, even if the results have not been great, ask yourself:

- Am I making this choice simply because this is what I always do in this situation and because it's the easiest for me?
- What other options are there? Can I think of 3-5 alternative options? Can I think of at least 1? If not, can Google or YouTube help me identify some?
- What would some of my friends or colleagues do in this situation?

- Would I be better off choosing something new rather than something familiar?
- What can I lose by trying something new in this case? Is there any risk at all?
- Can I afford to be wrong by trying something different?

NINE

Accepting What Is and Nothing Else

"Progress is impossible without change, and those who cannot change their minds cannot change anything."
George Bernard Shaw

Have you ever been in a job that you didn't like that much, but it was tolerable and allowed you to live a comfortable life? Were you ever in danger of losing that job? If you are like most people in this situation and don't have another job lined up already, your attitude towards your job may change instantly. The thought of losing those monthly paychecks becomes far more important than anything you dislike about the job. You likely put up a valiant fight with your company to keep your job. Whether you kept the job or not doesn't matter. What is important is to realize how much you wanted to preserve the status quo.

Status quo bias causes us to avoid change at all costs in order to maintain the current situation. We do this because we fear potential losses and stress, which the change could cause.

In most cases, our fear is not justified. Unfortunately, the fear we have of losing something outweighs our excitement about potential gains.

People have a tendency to want to keep things the way they are, even if it's not moving them forward, and even if it might cause them great harm in the long run. People prefer to keep things the way they are, rather than rocking the boat. Many of us simply assume things are better in their present state, even if they are not producing the results we want. This type of cognitive bias can directly affect personal behavior, while also having a larger impact on politics, economics, and social issues.

This is why so many issues in society can arise without people even realizing them until they become too big to ignore. When any changes do occur in the world, people who possess the status quo bias see it as a loss or detriment. For example, if an empty lot was turned into a shopping center, many individuals would be upset with the loss of land and not consider the new commercial development a positive change.

The status quo bias also affects our decision making skills. Countless studies by researchers have shown that people will choose options that keep things the way they are, especially when faced with a difficult choice. The status quo bias limits the chance of risk, but also causes people to miss out on benefits that outweigh the risk.[26]

There are many ways that the status quo bias is present throughout our society. If we pay attention, we can see it every day. For example, communities that suffer from poverty, crime, and other issues can implement solutions to improve their situation based on what other cities have done. But when these plans are considered for implementation, the community often rejects them because they would change too many things which the community is accustomed to. One of the plans may be to start a neighborhood watch program, but since many residents are wary of people watching them all the time like spies, they resist this plan despite the fact that it may reduce crime.

Politics and social issues are major examples of this cognitive bias at work. People complain about the people in power, yet they keep voting for those same people out of fear that someone else could make things even worse.

The status quo bias affects many personal decisions that we make on a daily basis. On one hand, we want to make progress in our lives, but on the other hand, we rarely make a genuine effort to move out of our comfort zone and change the status quo. Like with any other cognitive biases, some decisions affected by the status quo bias are small and will not have a major impact on our lives. For example, eating at the same restaurant, taking the same route to work, or always watching the same TV shows.

The status quo bias can also prevent us from changing services like our phone, cable, or internet service. Even when companies are getting expensive and have lackluster service, we will still refuse to switch service providers because we dislike the change more than the poor service.

There is one aspect of our lives where the status quo bias plays a very important but negative role, bad habits. Whether we eat too much, too often, and highly unhealthy foods or drink too much alcohol or not exercise enough, or not exercise at all, or work too much or not rest enough, we are often stuck in these bad habits and fail to break them. The longer we lived with a habit, the harder it is for us to stop it. And attempting to just stop a bad habit is usually a recipe for failure. A bad habit should always be replaced by a good one, instead of just stopping it, to maximize our chances of success. Because bad habits can damage and even ruin our health and our lives, we should always keep an eye on them and stop them in their tracks before they become entrenched in our brains.

The status quo bias can also affect our decisions and in business or our professional lives in very serious ways. It's very easy, for instance, to get stuck in the same job with the same company for many years and miss all the opportunities to move on to better jobs. Usually, when a new company moves into an area, they offer better salaries and benefits than the existing companies in order to attract employees. But, in spite of these better rewards, many people are still reluctant to leave their existing jobs and join the new company, preferring to stay in their lower paid jobs which they know inside out. However, people who move up the career ladder do so because they don't let their status quo bias control them. If you choose to stay in a job that is holding you back, merely because you know the routine, then you are making the conscious decision to not improve your circumstances.

On a different scale, there are many businesses losing out on profits and growth, simply because people running them are unwilling to change. Many large organizations have even gone out of business because they kept the same business practices that, although initially successful, became uncompetitive over time causing them harm and hemorrhaging money. Businesses need to grow out of their comfort zones to keep up with an ever changing world and to prosper. This includes constantly innovating and updating their products, figuring out novel ways to attract customers, and also keeping up with new laws that come into force.

Going back to the Covid-19 pandemic, many companies adjusted their practices because they knew they had to. If not, they would not have survived. In fact, many of them haven't. For some, the pandemic was the final nail in the coffin of a dying business. For others, their refusal to follow new policies, laws and public demands took them from a successful organization to certain bankruptcy. If the public is demanding new safety measures, then you must discard your status quo mindset and make all the necessary adjustments. The world is constantly changing and so must the companies.

Speaking of businesses, many people have good ideas for new and useful products and services which have the potential to turn into high-profit business ideas. Unfortunately, most of those people are too hesitant to act on their ideas. From youth, we are taught to go on the safe path that many before us did. However, the safe path will never lead to an exceptional life. For this to occur, the status quo mindset of doing what has always been done must be abandoned. If you have goals of becoming an entrepreneur, you must do what others who came before you did not.

Now let's discuss another issue in which the status quo bias can be a key factor, unhappy relationships. Some people are in a long-term relationship with the wrong partner, mostly because they are set in a familiar routine. Although these unhealthy relationships bring these people little to no joy, they are reluctant to break up and move on. Relationships like these are not exclusive to romantic partners. Friends, family members, and work associates can also be toxic to us, and yet we continue to spend time with them because it's what we've always done. It's difficult for us to break these associations because we cannot fathom change, even when we desperately need it.

Throughout life, we are held back by the belief that the default option is always the safe option. In many cases, this may be true, but there are so many opportunities that we miss out on with this mindset. Many businesses were never started because of fear. People missed out on traveling to dream destinations because they were unsure about it. Poor decisions have constantly been made because people were afraid of making better ones. While the status quo bias can be a form of self-protection, it also causes us to miss valuable opportunities.

The opposite of the status quo bias is **the fear of missing out**, also known as FOMO. If the status quo bias keeps you stuck in your current situation, which, by the way, feels comfortable and you don't see or refuse to see a good reason to change, FOMO acts as a catalyst for change, prompting you to take action. FOMO will be discussed in the next chapter.

Despite the countless negative effects mentioned above, the status quo bias can also play a very positive role in our lives. Because, when we live a healthy and happy life, surrounded by other happy people, we want to have a very strong status quo bias to help us maintain that bliss state of health and happiness.

Status Quo Bias in the Real World

In 1985, the first-ever Blockbuster Video store opened, and this organization quickly expanded to many cities around the US. Many people's weekends were set because they had a Blockbuster nearby. The video store giant seemed unstoppable during the 1990s and all the way into the mid-2000s. Unfortunately, Blockbuster made a huge blunder in the year 2000 by sticking to its classic methods of video rental and not getting in quick enough on the online streaming revolution.

In 2000, the founder of Netflix, Reed Hastings, flew to Dallas to have a meeting with Blockbuster CEO John Antioco and his team. He proposed that the two companies could join forces and Netflix would run Blockbuster's brand online. This idea did not go over well and Hastings was laughed out of the room.

Well, Hastings got the last laugh because Netflix is worth billions, while Blockbuster is out of business. Well, except for one store in Bend, OR. Of course, it's hard to blame Blockbuster because the internet was not nearly as big in 2000 as it is now, and Netflix was a fledgling company at the time. They could have used the idea of Netflix to start something new, but the Blockbuster CEO did not see the company moving past video rentals at the time. Sticking to what worked in the 90s was his method for success.

Blockbuster eventually gained competition from Redbox, and then Netflix eventually took off. All of this left Blockbuster in the dust. The movie rental giant did eventually get in on the online revolution, but it was way too late by then.[27]

Overcoming the Status Quo Bias

The status quo bias is a limiting mindset that leads to a pattern of thinking that reinforces the current, usual way of doing things. If we are striving to reach higher levels of success in our lives, then this mindset must be shattered. Stop doing things simply because that's how you've always done them. Traditions have been broken before. If people throughout history just accepted the status quo, then much of the progress and inventions we have made never would have seen the light of day. If you are ready to make your own history, then it's time to embrace change, rather than maintain the status quo.

. . .

ACKNOWLEDGE **The Need To Change**

The greatest challenge we have in this area is accepting that we need to improve in order to avoid being left behind by our peers, competitors, friends and everyone else that matters. Many successful people develop an inflated view of themselves and become arrogant once they have achieved a high level of success. Their judgment becomes very subjective as they start believing they already know everything there is to know in their professional or personal life and become stubborn about any changes suggested by others.

SEEK **Feedback**

It is important to seek and be open to feedback from others, at least once in a while. Getting an objective opinion about our strengths and weaknesses is very useful indeed. We are often blind to our own faults, so getting an outside perspective can help us improve ourselves. Ask a few people who know you well for "constructive criticism" about yourself. Ask them to help you identify the areas in your life which you should improve. Then look for patterns in their answers to determine the most important things you need to change. To avoid any confusion, always confirm with those people that your understanding of their feedback is accurate.

DEFINE **Your Goal And Learn How To Best Achieve It**

Once you have understood the feedback and have decided to act on it, it's important to define your goal or goals so you are crystal clear about what success looks like in this case. Then you need to research and learn how to best achieve it. There are many ways to do this, but regardless of how you do your research, it's important to make sure you have access to the most up-to-date information. Blogs, books, podcasts, Facebook groups, YouTube videos, and online training programs are all very useful for learning how to best achieve your goal. You just need to find the right source for your needs. If the change is small, watching a few YouTube videos may be enough. If it's significant, then an online training program coupled with a Facebook group may be the right way to go about it.

STAY Motivated Throughout The Change Process

Change is often difficult, which is why so many people get stuck in a status quo. But if you are clear about "what" needs to change and "why", and know the "how", then you just need to keep your motivation high and keep moving forward until you achieve your goal. To improve your chances to stay motivated when change is tough is best to join a support group or hire a personal coach. This way, you will feel accountable for taking positive actions and also get timely advice on how to overcome any unexpected obstacles.

To experience growth, improve your circumstances, and reach your full potential, you must be ready to reject the status quo when necessary. Do your best to overcome the status quo biases when they harm you or prevent you from making progress, but make those biases strong when they help you protect your gains or maintain the positive aspects of your life.

Stop and Think

When you find yourself stuck in the same place or in same routines, ask yourself:

- Have I become completely reluctant to change?

- Am I resistant to trying new ways of doing things or having new experiences?
- Are there any new tools and methods which could help me become better and more productive?
- Are there any new things which I could try that could improve the quality of my life?

TEN

Feeling Left Out

"For everything you have missed, you have gained something else."
Ralph Waldo Emerson

Have you ever come across a very exciting offer for a product or service which was going to expire soon and you just couldn't resist it? Did you discover later on that it wasn't that special or time-limited after all? This is a situation that is all too familiar to many of us.

Do you also feel like you are constantly missing out on the fun things in life? It's as if no matter where you are, the exciting events are always happening at a different location altogether. This can produce an anxious or depressed feeling because you feel like you are being left out. This phenomenon has a name. It's actually called **'Fear of Missing Out', or 'FOMO'**.

FOMO is an anxiety triggered by the thought that you could be missing an exciting experience or important opportunity. "It is the fear that deciding not to participate is the wrong choice".[28] As a result of this mindset, people will try to participate in anything and everything they can, even if they don't actually enjoy it.

This is a very common occurrence, and it is becoming much more prevalent since it's so easy to see what's going on in the world. FOMO is a very significant cause of stress. We have a perception that other people are living much better lives than we do. This perception is based on our limited knowledge of what is really happening, and the fear derived from this perception. This feeling is based on our opinion about what has been seen or heard, rather than actual evidence or experience.

FOMO goes way beyond just thinking there are better options available in the world. It is specifically the feeling that we are missing out on an important event that you can't afford to miss but have no idea how to experience it. These feelings create a lot of jealousy and reduce our self-esteem.

There are many examples of this. Your friend may be having a celebration that you cannot attend. As a result, you feel as though you're missing out on the party of the century. It does not matter what you are doing at that moment, the event you are missing always seems more important. A person who suffers from FOMO literally wants to be in a different place doing something else and can perceive themselves as a failure if they aren't.

This mindset of missing out can impact the business world too. FOMO causes companies to lose focus by constantly trying to keep up with the latest trends in their industry. Instead of doing their own research, they jump on an idea quickly while it's new and exciting. If the trend loses its steam or was never a productive idea to begin with, then the company can lose money and even go bankrupt.

FOMO could also be very dangerous for start-ups if they rush to adopt new products or systems that have not proven their worth. Start-ups often have low capital at the outset, so jumping on an unproven trend simply because others are doing it can prove to be financially detrimental. Your start-up might end up dying before it gets a chance to get started.

FOMO also causes people to spend their money on expensive 'make money online' programs that promise easy ways to make money. Watching a guy next to a brand new Ferrari, or on a yacht, or in front of a mansion promoting his make easy money program can certainly get you very excited. The reality, however, is that these programs either don't work at all, or they only work for a small fraction of people because a significant amount of effort, patience, and additional funds are needed for success. Unless you are lucky, there is no easy way to make money. Always be skeptical and do your own research before jumping on one of these. Examples of these online ventures include affiliate marketing, digital marketing agencies, consulting, drop-shipping, etc. The people who are most likely to make money on these programs are the ones who are promoting them.

Essentially, this is a bias where you always feel your life is inferior. This mindset seems to be growing, and it is hardly something new. This ubiquitous feeling has been around for generations, but we are learning more about the science behind it. We now realize it's an actual phenomenon that keeps people from living their lives fully.

Based on many historical texts, we know FOMO has been around in some form for several centuries. People have always thought that someone else is living a better life than they are. This thought process has been studied in depth since the mid-1990s. The term was first coined by Dr. Dan Herman, who is a marketing strategist. During the earlier years of its discovery, FOMO was occurring on a smaller scale because of the reduced connection people had with the world. At that time, people barely even knew what their neighbors were doing or what was going on in the world. They did not have instant access to people's lives 24/7, like we do now.

Before the internet and its various platforms took off, individuals would see what their neighbors, friends, coworkers and various family members were doing. In many cases, they would feel their lives to be inferior, based on direct comparisons. When friends would have an event going on that they could not attend, they would feel a sense of loss and isolation.

As various social media platforms started growing, everyone had instant access to people's lives. The ability to compare your life to someone else's grew exponentially. This accelerated FOMO in many ways. You get a skewed view of what is happening in the world because people are showcasing the high points in their lives on social media and not the normal or negative aspects. This creates a feeling that the lives of others are much better or perfect, while ours are boring and unproductive.

People in every age category use social media platforms to a certain degree. However, teens and young adults practically live on them and have had access to them for most of their lives. It's easy to see then that FOMO affects younger people the most. Older generations have lived and experienced much of their lives, while younger adults have not seen as much. They often define how good their lives are by how many different experiences they have had. If they believe that they are missing out on specific experiences, then the feelings of missing out can show themselves through anxiety and depression.

FOMO is one of the reasons social media leads to many different mood disorders. Research is being done to understand it and help overcome it. A study done by the National Institute of Health, involving 1,800 participants, showed that the people who used social media the most within the group were 2.7 times more likely to have depression than those who used it the least. This study was published in the Journal of Depression and Anxiety. Perpetually living vicariously through the lives of others has dire consequences.

It is a vicious cycle. The use of social media leads to FOMO. FOMO can lead to mood disorders. These mood disorders lead to more social media use. The ironic part here is that people often exaggerate or even lie on social media, so our feelings of missing out are based on false information. Some people will fudge a few experiences here or there, like giving everyone the false impression that they are exercising regularly or constantly travel to nice places. In a study conducted by custard.com, only 18% of men and 19% of women reported an accurate profile on their Facebook pages.[29] The next time you get jealous of someone on social media, make sure that you realize that you are not seeing the real version of their lives.

The FOMO bias makes you miss making the most of your life experience because you are always distracted by something else. Since this bias causes you to be more focused on other people and things, you will inevitably make poor decisions about your own life. In reality, you will ignore most of your own life. Because FOMO can be a very dangerous mindset if you don't monitor it and manage it properly, it's imperative to change your thought process before your entire life passes you by.

It's important to note that in spite of all the negative effects mentioned above, FOMO can actually be used in a positive way too, as the driving force for positive change in your life. By using FOMO to your advantage, you can, for example, change your career from a boring one with an uncertain future to a much more exciting one which is also future proof.

The opposite of FOMO is **the status quo bias**. As discussed in the previous chapter, when you are affected by the status quo bias, instead of being eager to change, you feel comfortable in your current situation and don't see any good reason to change at all.

A similar bias to FOMO is called **the shiny object syndrome**. The main difference between the two is that while FOMO causes you to buy or invest in something completely new to you or your business, the shiny object syndrome causes you to chase apparently better versions of something you have already.

The shiny object syndrome is the exact opposite of the sunk cost fallacy, discussed in Chapter 2. If the sunk cost fallacy causes someone to stick to bad investments, the shiny object syndrome affects a person's ability to focus on their initial goals, prompting them to go for something that is perceived to be better. While it's good to always improve, you should not simply go after something and then forget about it before you give it a real chance. You will never reach your goals this way. This would be like buying a guitar and guitar lessons, but then getting excited about the piano and ditching the guitar before even really trying it out.

In business, it is imperative to focus on specific projects and see them to completion. When you behave in this manner, you will be more productive and reach your goals. Unfortunately, so many business owners always go after the new shiny object, rather than focusing on and improving what they already have. They don't realize that what they have is more than enough.

For example, a small business owner might start using an online program that is simple, but able to keep track of finances, including payroll and inventory. Although satisfied with this program, they may come across a newer program that is more expensive but supposedly far more advanced too. If this business owner has the shiny object syndrome, then they will probably ditch the simple program and move on to the supposedly better option even if they don't actually need any of the new advanced features and functionality because they were not intended for his type of business in the first place. What happens when another shiny program comes to market? Will the business owner buy this newer shiny program just for the sake of using the latest technology? When dealing with the shiny object syndrome, you need to assess if the new thing that you're chasing is truly better than what you already have, and also if acquiring this shiny object makes any sense at all.

Picture an actress who gets a minor role in a new Netflix series. While she is rehearsing for it, a more appealing role comes up, but she can't do both. So, she quickly decides to abandon the current role and go after the more exciting one instead. However, shortly after starting the rehearsals for this newer role, she realizes that it is not what she had imagined at all. She regrets her move, which was based on a very little information, but it's too late to reverse her decision. Remember, just because something looks more satisfying, does not mean that it is. Do your homework before making any hasty decisions.

The opposite of the shiny object syndrome is **the sunk cost fallacy**. When you are affected by the sunk cost fallacy, you feel stuck because you are too invested in your current situation or project, as discussed in Chapter 2. Whereas, when you are affected by the shiny object syndrome, you don't care at all about abandoning your current situation or project, regardless of how much you have invested already, because you are now in pursuit of something that seems far more promising.

FOMO in the Real World

You may have heard of boxing great Evander Holyfield. While this athlete was legendary in the ring, it did not translate into success with his finances. Despite making hundreds of millions of dollars during his illustrious career, at one point he ended up having to give up his mansion in Atlanta and sell all of his memorabilia to survive.

How did this happen? Well, going through two divorces did not help. In addition, Mr. Holyfield invested and lost millions of dollars on failed business ventures that seemed hot at the time, like a restaurant chain and a record label. However, the ventures were a complete flop as Mr. Holyfield got into them too quickly without doing the proper research. Buying popular but unnecessary items, like overpriced cars and the mansion I mentioned earlier, also led to the pugilist's financial woes. Mr. Holyfield admits having poor money practices and no one around to guide him, and this eventually caused him to lose over 300 million dollars of his fortune. He insists he can make up for it someday. Holyfield was never one to give up, so it could happen.[30]

On a similar note, one of Evander Holyfield's rivals, Mike Tyson, had similar financial issues due to jumping on the latest trends and constantly buying expensive items, like jewelry, clothing, cars, houses, and even tigers. Instead of saving and investing his money, he spent it on whatever new trend or toy he could get his hands on. It is estimated that Tyson made over

400 million dollars during his career, but eventually went bankrupt in the early 2000s.

Instead of focusing on what we don't have, it would do most of us well to focus on what we do have. The grass is not always greener on the other side. Try enjoying your own grass.

Overcoming FOMO

Fortunately for us, we can curb the effects of FOMO and start living our own lives. It's time to stop caring so much about what everyone else is doing. The following steps can help with your progress.

START JOURNALING

Some of us use social media as a new form of journaling, but this isn't ideal for two reasons. Firstly, you will most likely be influenced by how many people like and react to what you post. Secondly, you will most likely censor yourself to avoid embarrassing yourself. Thus, you won't reap the full benefits of writing a *personal, private* journal. Personal journaling shifts your attention from public approval to self-appreciation and will most definitely help you clear your thoughts and avoid making rush decisions.

MAKE GRATITUDE A **Daily Habit**

FOMO is prevalent in people who are too focused on what they lack in their lives. Shift your attention and start being grateful for the good things you have already. Studies have shown that being grateful for the good things in your life can significantly improve your overall perspective. When you are focused on the abundance that you have, you will attract more good things in your life. You should also consider starting a gratitude journal in order to help you not only cultivate but also make the most of this habit.

SURROUND **Yourself With Supportive People**

Make sure you are surrounded by positive and supportive people. Become friends with those who compliment you and point out your strong sides. Don't spend time around people who are too negative or always compare you to others in a negative, non constructive, way.

LIMIT **Your Time On Passive Social Media**

Use social media mainly to interact with people rather than just for watching what other people do. Seek out real connections with real people instead. Reach out to colleagues, friends and family and talk to them. If you feel isolated, take up a new hobby that involves social interaction and also consider going out somewhere by yourself on a more regular basis, just to be around other people.

GET **Into The Habit Of Finishing What You Start**

You should cultivate the habit of finishing the things that you start before moving on to something else. Getting things done will give you a sense of accomplishment, will increase your confidence levels, and most importantly will increase your chances of success when undertaking similar tasks or projects in the future. Although it's not always possible or practical to finish what you start, the more things you complete, the better you will become at getting things done. To build this habit over time, start with the small activities or tasks, such as tidying a room, organizing a bookshelf, writing an email, etc., and then move on to more complex and time consuming activities. For complex projects, it's important to create a high level project plan, so that you are crystal clear about what needs to be done and when. It's also important to define the key milestones and celebrate achieving them. This habit of getting things done will prevent you from constantly switching from one project to the next without ever accomplishing anything meaningful.

ALWAYS VALIDATE **The Implied Assumptions**

We tend to get excited about the most promising opportunities and completely forget to validate even the most basic assumptions before committing our time and money to a new endeavor. However, if something seems too good to be true, it very often is. So, before committing to a so called 'life changing' course of action, write down all the critical success factors that you are aware of. These can be assumptions about the skills, knowledge and experience necessary for success and be perfectly honest with yourself if you have them or not. Additionally, always find out all the hidden fees and costs and quantify any additional time and money investments required for success. Basically, you need to confirm that all the implied assumptions are true in your particular case and that your expectations are realistic and within your reach. It's just too easy to jump on an exciting opportunity out of FOMO, only to find out later that it wasn't right for you at all.

FOMO is not something you should take lightly because it can create unexpected problems and complications in your life.

However, keep in mind that used wisely, FOMO can help you change your life in very positive and meaningful ways.

Stop and Think

When you are very excited about a limited time offer or don't want to miss an opportunity, it can create a lot of pressure to make a decision. This can happen when we consider making purchases of products or services. In these cases, FOMO can cause us to make unwise decisions. When you are in these situations, ask yourself:

- Is this really a good deal, or it just seems so because I haven't looked for any other options yet?
- What alternatives are there and how do they compare?
- How easy is it to get a refund?
- Is this too good to be true?
- Could this be a scam? If it was a scam, how would it work?
- How can I protect myself and limit my losses?
- Do I trust this company? How long have they been in business for?

ELEVEN

Stop and Think Questions

This chapter contains all the Stop and Think questions from the entire book in one single place for easy reference.

Overconfidence (Chapter 1)

When you are on a winning streak, going from one success to another, getting everything right, and about to make a very important decision, ask yourself:

- What exactly makes me feel so sure that I am making the right decision now?
- Is my decision based on sufficient and relevant information?
- Am I cutting any corners or jumping to conclusions?
- Who can I speak to in order to validate my assumptions?
- Do I know all the potential risks?
- Does anyone disagree with me? Do they have a valid point? Have I dismissed their views too quickly and without proper consideration?

- Are there any hidden costs or additional costs further down the line that I am not aware of?
- Is there anything important that I could be missing?
- Do I have enough experience and knowledge to make an informed decision in this particular instance?

Sunk-Cost Fallacy (Chapter 2)

When you are in a situation where investing more money and/or time brings you no further benefits and it could even hurt you, ask yourself:

- Why am I doing this, anyway? Is it for the sake of the money and time I have invested already?
- Would I be better off by cutting my losses and moving on?
- What other opportunities would I miss by sticking to this path?

As a matter of principle, try to avoid making a bad investment even worse by investing any additional resources like money or time.

Confirmation Bias (Chapter 3)

When you come across a new piece of information that contradicts one of your existing beliefs, ask yourself:

- Is this true?
- Can I trust this source?
- How significant is this new piece of information?
- Does it change anything at all?
- Who is going to win and who is going to lose if this is true?

- Could anyone lose their power, job or reputation based on this information?
- Would anyone's ego get seriously hurt?

When everything that you hear or read about a topic you care about reinforces what you already believed to be true, ask yourself:

- Is this the full picture or just carefully cropped out version of the truth that people keep repeating without much thinking?
- What if all these people are wrong?
- Can the opposite be true?
- Are my assumptions still true today?
- What is the actual proof that my beliefs are right?
- Who disagrees with my beliefs and why?
- Has anything changed since I made my mind up about this?
- Why exactly do I believe things as I do?

False Dichotomies (Chapter 4)

When you are facing a choice between only two options, ask yourself:

- Is this really a black or white situation?
- Could this be a false dichotomy or a false dilemma instead?
- How much do I trust the information I have?
- Could other options be possible?
- Do I really have to make a decision now or can I delay it?
- Will I risk missing an opportunity if I take more time

to decide? How likely is this risk? How big is the opportunity?
- How much time can I afford to spend searching for other options?

Endowment Effect (Chapter 5)

When trying to sell a product or a service that you own, ask yourself:

- Am I overpricing my product or service just because it's mine?
- Why would anyone pay the price I am asking for? Is there anything unique about it? Is it scarce?
- What is the current price for this product or service, or for similar ones?
- Where can I get a realistic valuation for it?
- Will I risk missing a window of opportunity if I overprice this product or service?

Halo Effect (Chapter 6)

When someone who is an expert in one field ventures into a new field, or a company launches products or services which are different from what they are usually known for, ask yourself:

- Does this make any sense at all?
- Have other people or companies been successful in similar scenarios?
- Can this person or company really be successful with this new endeavor in the long run?
- How do they describe their decision to use their position to influence others?
- Are you allowing yourself to be influenced by

someone's opinion without knowing the actual facts behind the issue or topic?
- Am I judging this person based on superficial aspects such as looks, income or fame?
- Do I have an opportunity to learn more about this person or thing before I decide if their opinion is valuable to me?

Correlation and Causation (Chapter 7)

When two factors, let's call them A and B, are correlated, ask yourself?

- How do I know for sure that A has been caused by B? What proof do I have?
- What if B has been caused by A instead? Is there any proof for this?
- Is it possible that both A and B have been caused by a hidden factor C?
- Is it possible that there is no cause-and-effect relationship between A and B?

Familiarity Bias (Chapter 8)

When you are faced with situations that are familiar to you and your natural instinct is to do what you've always done, even if the results have not been great, ask yourself:

- Am I making this choice simply because this is what I always do in this situation and because it's the easiest for me?
- What other options are there? Can I think of 3-5 alternative options? Can I think of at least 1? If not, can Google or YouTube help me identify some?

- What would some of my friends or colleagues do in this situation?
- Would I be better off choosing something new rather than something familiar?
- What can I lose by trying something new in this case? Is there any risk at all?
- Can I afford to be wrong by trying something different?

Status Quo Bias (Chapter 9)

When you find yourself stuck in the same place or in same routines, ask yourself:

- Have I become completely reluctant to change?
- Am I resistant to trying new ways of doing things or having new experiences?
- Are there any new tools and methods which could help me become better and more productive?
- Are there any new things which I could try that could improve the quality of my life?

Fear of Missing Out, a.k.a. FOMO (Chapter 10)

When you are very excited about a limited time offer or don't want to miss an opportunity, it can create a lot of pressure to make a decision. This can happen when we consider making purchases of products or services. In these cases, FOMO can cause us to make unwise decisions. When you are in these situations, ask yourself:

- Is this really a good deal, or it just seems so because I haven't looked for any other options yet?

Stop and Think Questions

- What alternatives are there and how do they compare?
- How easy is it to get a refund?
- Is this too good to be true?
- Could this be a scam? If it was a scam, how would it work?
- How can I protect myself and limit my losses?
- Do I trust this company? How long have they been in business for?

Conclusion

While reading this book and learning about the various cognitive biases, chances are that you recognized them within yourself or someone you know well. Most people are not aware of these biases and of how they influence our decisions. We are so busy living our day-to-day lives, rushing from one thing to another, that we rarely stop to reflect on the decisions that don't go as planned and on how we can improve our thinking to make better decisions. The most important thing is to recognize the cognitive biases first. After this, you must take active steps to prevent them from influencing you. If you do this consistently, you will see many positive changes in your life for sure.

Every time you face an important decision, I encourage you to refer to Chapter 11, which summarizes all the Stop and Think questions for the ten main cognitive biases covered in the book, and do a quick check to see if any of them could influence the decision you are about to make. If that's the case, then answer all the Stop and Think questions for that bias before making the actual decision. You may also want to read the Overcoming the Bias section in the chapter that covers that particular cognitive bias for additional details on how to prevent the bias from interfering with your decision. This shouldn't take more than a few minutes, but it's time worth spending.

To improve your decision making skills further, you should always reflect on your past decisions, learn from your mistakes and celebrate your successes. And you should always give yourself credit when you have successfully avoided making a bad decision by overcoming a cognitive bias.

My promises to you at the beginning of this book were to show you how different cognitive biases affect our thinking and influence our decisions in our personal and professional lives, and also to show you how to overcome these biases and avoid making poor decisions because of them. I hope that I have delivered on these promises, and that this book has given you new perspectives and tools that you can use to overcome your cognitive biases and to make effective decisions that lead you to new heights of success in every area of your life.

As a departing thought, here is a useful quote that you should always remember:

"Sometimes it's the smallest decisions that can change your life forever." - Keri Russell

Thanks for reading Thinking Guide for Busy People.

If you enjoyed the book, it would really mean a lot to me if you could leave a brief and honest review on Amazon, or any other online bookshop or book club, to help others discover and benefit from the book. Reviews are very important for independent authors like myself, and if you could spare a minute to write a line or two about what you liked the most about the book, I would highly appreciate it. Thanks in advance for your kind support!

References

1. Ribeiro, P.C. (2012, August 2). Sinking the Unsinkable: Lessons for Leadership. Appel.NASA.gov. (Ribeiro, 2012)
2. Road Safety Annual Report USA 2019 (2019). International Transport Forum. ITF-OECD.org.
3. The Guardian (2020, April 12). PM's Covid-19 timeline: from 'mild symptoms' to a brush with death. TheGuardian.com.
4. NexChange. (2017, May 4). Descendant of One of America's Founding Fathers Loses Billions Investing in Fintech Startups. NexChangeNOW.com
5. McRaney, D. (2011, March 25). The Sunk Cost Fallacy. YouAreNotSoSmart.com. (McRaney, 2011)
6. Slotnick, D. (2019, October 7). The history of the Concorde supersonic jet - BusinessInsider.com. (Slotnick, 2019)
7. Confirmation bias. (2016). ScienceDaily.com.
8. False Dilemma. (n.d.). www.LogicallyFallacious.com
9. Ward, T. (2017, April 29). The Amazing Story Of The Making Of "Rocky." Forbes.com. (Ward, 2017)

10. The Doc. (2019). 34 Great Scientists Who Were Committed Christians. FamousScientists.org.
11. Ganti, A. (2019, August 16). Endowment Effect Definition. Investopedia.com. (Ganti, 2019)
12. Utaraitė, N. (2020, September). 20 Fateful Times People Happened Across Random Things That Turned Out To Be Worth A Fortune. BoredPanda.com. (Utaraitė, 2020)
13. Mohammed, S. (2019, May 27). Endowment Effect in Business and Marketing. Medium.com. (Mohammed, 2019)
14. Wikipedia Contributors. (2019, April 18). Halo effect. Wikipedia.org.
15. Lisa, A. (2020, September 17). Celebrity Endorsement Deals With Insane Payouts. Yahoo Finance. finance.yahoo.com. (Lisa, 2020)
16. Pasley, J. (n.d.). The rise and fall of XFL — Vince McMahon's wild, sexualized, exaggerated answer to football that lasted only one season. BusinessInsider.com. (Pasley, n.d.)
17. Chiasson, B. (2015, August 21). What is a false-causality fallacy? - Quora.com. (Chiasson, 2015)
18. Maslow, J. (2019, March 12). 20% of Serious Medical Conditions are Misdiagnosed, Study Finds. LegalScoops.com. (Maslow, 2019)
19. Innocence Project (2018) . Malcolm Alexander. InnocenceProject.org.
20. Wikipedia Contributors. (2020, September 21). Miscarriage of justice. Wikipedia.org.
21. ONS (2020, August 12). GDP first quarterly estimate, UK: April to June 2020. Office for National Statistics. ONS.gov.uk. (ONS, 2020)
22. Ong, J. (2020, April 20). The 10 Worst Roles On

Robert Pattinson's IMDb Page (And 5 Best). TheThings.com. (Ong, 2020)
23. Ricciardi, V., & Baker, H. K. (2014, June 23). (PDF) How Biases Affect Investor Behaviour. ResearchGate.net. (Ricciardi & Baker, 2014)
24. Ledsom, A. (2020, August 4). Virgin Galactic Says Space Holidays Possible By Early 2021–Tickets Are $250,000. Forbes.com. (Ledsom, 2020)
25. Dan, A. (2012, January 23). Kodak Failed By Asking The Wrong Marketing Question. Forbes.com. (Dan, 2012)
26. Cherry, K. (2020, May 11). How the Status Quo Bias Influences the Decisions You Make. VeryWellMind.com. (Cherry, 2020)
27. Satell, G. (n.d.). A Look Back At Why Blockbuster Really Failed And Why It Didn't Have To. Forbes.com. (Satell, n.d.)
28. Rouse, M. (n.d.). What is FOMO (fear of missing out)? Definition. WhatIs.com. (Rouse, n.d.)
29. Warren, C. (2018, July 30). How Honest Are People on Social Media? PsychologyToday.com. (Warren, 2018)
30. Savage, N. (2019, November 14). How Boxing legend Evander Holyfield blew $300 million. News.Com.Au. (Savage, 2019)

www.ingramcontent.com/pod-product-compliance
Lightning Source LLC
Chambersburg PA
CBHW031429210526
45464CB00005B/2110